NHS HEALTH ADVISORY SERVICE
THEMATIC REVIEW

SUICIDE PREVENTION

THE CHALLENGE CONFRONTED

A MANUAL OF GUIDANCE FOR

THE PURCHASERS AND PROVIDERS

OF MENTAL HEALTH CARE

Editors

Dr Richard Williams and Professor H Gethin Morgan

Authors

Professor H Gethin Morgan

Dr John Coleman

Mr Michael Farrar

Professor Peter Hill

Professor Michael Kerfoot

Dr Richard Williams

Sub-editor

Mrs Jenny Croft

LONDON: HMSO

Foreword

Suicide is a major cause of preventable death in England, which is why we have set targets for suicide reduction in the Government's Health of the Nation White Paper. In 1992 there were 5,542 cases of known suicide in England. This contrasts with 3,814 killed on the roads in 1993. I am therefore very pleased that this, the first Thematic Review by the NHS Health Advisory Service, should be aimed at tackling the problem.

The Review comprises a practical guide, mainly aimed at providers of secondary health care, on how best to approach the problem at the individual level. It is not only about what to do, but about how to go about it. It therefore represents a practical step to tackling this growing problem. In particular, it is founded on the belief that it is feasible to prevent at least some suicides and that this message should be carried to those in a position to help individuals.

At a personal level, suicide is a terrible needless tragedy. I hope and believe that this document will help raise awareness of how to avoid such tragedies and contribute towards achieving a significant reduction in suicide rates.

Virginia Bottomley
Secretary of State for Health
Whitehall
LONDON

July 1994

The Editors and Authors

Dr John Coleman

Dr John Coleman trained as a clinical psychologist at the Middlesex Hospital, London. He worked for 14 years as a Senior Lecturer in the Department of Psychiatry in the Royal London Hospital. Since 1988, he has been the Director of the Trust for the Study of Adolescence, an independent research and training organisation based in Brighton. He is currently the Editor of the Journal of Adolescence and the Editor of the Routledge book series 'Adolescence and Society'. He has published a number of books, the most well-known being 'The Nature of Adolescence', now in its second edition. He is a Fellow of the British Psychological Society and acts as a consultant for many organisations, including the World Health Organisation and The Prince's Trust.

Mrs Jenny Croft

Mrs Jenny Croft joined the then Department of Health and Social Security after reading English at Oxford. She worked on both sides of that Department in a range of jobs including: nurse training and the legislation to establish the UK Central Council for Nursing, Midwifery, and Health Visiting: regional liaison: and she was Secretary to the Warnock Inquiry into Human Fertilisation and Embryology. After a period of secondment to the Cabinet Office, where she worked for the Civil Service Selection Board, she gave up full-time work to bring up a family. Since then she has undertaken work on a freelance basis for the Department of Health.

Mr Mike Farrar

Mr Mike Farrar is the Mental Health Strategy Manager for the Northern and Yorkshire Regional Health Authority. He is currently seconded to the Performance Management Directorate, in the National Health Service Executive in Leeds. He is a social sciences graduate from Nottingham University who has pursued a varied career in both the public and private sector undertaking managerial, research and development and strategic planning roles. He has focused particularly on services for people with mental health or addiction problems and has been based predominantly in the north of England. In recent years, he has also been a member of the Director's advisory panel for the NHS Health Advisory Service Thematic Review of Child and Adolescent Mental Health Services and, in 1993, a member of the NHS Health Advisory Service/Mental Health Act Commission/Social Services Inspectorate Review Team on Adolescent Forensic Psychiatry Services.

Professor Peter Hill

Professor Peter Hill is Head of the Section of Child Mental Health at St George's Hospital Medical School, London, and a Consultant Child and Adolescent Psychiatrist at St George's Hospital. He chairs the specialist Section on Child and Adolescent Psychiatry of the Royal College of Psychiatrists. Until recently, most of his academic work was concerned with teaching, examining and writing but its current pattern is increasingly dominated by research into adolescent psychiatry service evaluation and problems associated with sleep and disability in childhood. The author or editor of three published textbooks of psychiatry and adolescent psychiatry, he is collaborating with Professor David Hull on a book on childhood disability.

Professor Michael Kerfoot

Professor Michael Kerfoot is the newly appointed Professor of Child and Adolescent Policy and Research in the School of

Psychiatry and Behavioural Sciences, University of Manchester. He is also Co-Director of the Mental Health Social Work Research and Staff Development Unit. He has 16 years experience of working in child and adolescent mental health services in Liverpool, Newcastle, and Manchester. His main research interest has been in adolescent suicidal behaviour. He has published widely in this field, both nationally and internationally, and has been a regular contributor to conferences both in the UK and abroad. He has twice been a visiting Research Associate at the Los Angeles Suicide Prevention Centre, and is an Honorary Consultant to the Samaritans.

Professor H Gethin Morgan

Professor Gethin Morgan has been the Norah Hurle Cooke Professor of Mental Health in the University of Bristol since 1979. Prior to that, and as Consultant Senior Lecturer from 1968, he developed a particular interest in non-fatal deliberate self-harm and suicide. His book, 'Death Wishes: the Understanding and Management of Deliberate Self Harm', published in 1979, summarised a decade of research in this field. Since then, he has focused his research on suicide in psychiatric patients and the prevention of repetition of non-fatal self-harm. His work emphasises the importance of establishing high standards of clinical care for suicidal people and the need

to accord due importance to aiming at modest, indirect goals at first, in the search for effective strategies in suicide prevention.

Dr Richard Williams

Dr Richard Williams is the present Director of the NHS Health Advisory Service (HAS). Upon appointment in 1992, he was required to reposition the HAS so that it could exercise its remit within the reformed health service. One of the new activities of the HAS which he has developed is the Thematic Review, of which the HAS has seven in progress.

He is also a Consultant Child and Adolescent Psychiatrist at the Bristol Royal Hospital for Sick Children where he developed an extensive liaison and consultation practice with other community child care workers and the child health services. His particular clinical interests include the psychological impacts and treatment of life-threatening and chronic physical disorders and the immediate and long-term management of psychological trauma in families.

Outside his clinical role and throughout the past 12 years, he has developed specialised experience in selecting and training leaders. He has been involved in service management and, consequent on his work with the HAS, has gained particular experience with the challenges posed to health and local authorities in commissioning comprehensive health services for mentally ill and elderly people.

Contents

Chapter One

Introduction

1.1 This volume is presented in response to three opportunities: enactment of the new roles of the NHS Health Advisory Service (HAS); exercising the extension of the HAS remit given to it in 1993 by Ministers; seizing the opportunity to bring together professional developments in the field of suicide prevention and the Government's Health of the Nation[1] strategic initiative.

The NHS Health Advisory Service (HAS)

1.2 Established as the Hospital Advisory Service in 1969, the HAS has retained its core remit, which is that of contributing to the maintenance and improvement of the quality of management, organisation and standards of delivery of patient care, mainly for elderly and mentally ill people. Over 25 years, the HAS has developed the capacity to act as the 'eyes and ears'[2] of the Secretaries of State for Health and for Wales. It was reviewed by Ministers in 1991 and the outcome was a requirement that I should adjust the roles of the HAS to take account of the NHS reforms. Included in the new and more focused missions given by Ministers was the requirement that the HAS should accept commissions relating to specific themes on a national basis and this gave rise to the concept of *Thematic Reviews*.[3] The HAS has seven such reviews in preparation and this is the first to reach publication.

1.3 Additionally, in 1993, Ministers extended the remit of the HAS by giving it explicit responsibilities for monitoring the quality of health care and the performance of purchasers. So, this Thematic Review offers advice to both the purchasers and providers of mental health services.

The Health of the Nation Mental Illness Key Area

1.4 In 1992, the Health of the Nation White Paper launched a strategic health initiative in England. It selected five Key Areas of which one is mental illness. Objectives and targets were set in each key area and the White Paper set a framework for initiation, development, monitoring and review of the strategy. The **objective of the mental illness key area is that of reducing ill-health and death caused by mental illness.** The targets are:

Table One – England

To improve significantly the health and social functioning of mentally ill people.
To reduce the overall suicide rate by at least 15% by the year 2000 (from 11.1 per 100,000 population in 1990 to no more than 9.4).
To reduce the suicide rate of severely mentally ill people by at least 33% by the year 2000 (from the estimate of 15% in 1990 to no more than 10%).
These figures represent suicide and self-inflicted injury (ICD E950-E959) and injury undetermined whether accidentally or purposely inflicted (ICD 980-989).

These targets are reproduced for ease of reference in Check-List 1 (page 102).

Mental Illness Services – A Strategy for Wales

1.5 In 1989, Wales adopted a specific mental health strategy in the form of the Welsh Office initiative entitled Mental

---

[1] Department of Health, 1992.

[2] Crossman, R. Diaries, 1977.

[3] NHS Health Advisory Service, 1993.

Illness Services – A Strategy for Wales. Subsequently, in 1993 the Welsh Health Planning Forum drew up a Protocol for Investment in Health Gain – Mental Health. It has three overall goals which relate directly and indirectly to suicide.

Table One – Wales

To increase the proportion of those with a severe mental illness who have a permanent home with appropriate levels of support to 75% by 1997 and 90% by 2002.

To reduce the overall suicide rate by at least 15% by the year 2002 (baseline 1991: males 13.7 and females 3.6 per 100,000 population).

To reduce the suicide rate of severely mentally ill people by at least 33% by the year 2002.

These tables are reproduced for ease of reference in Check-List 1 (page 102).

The NHS Health Advisory Service Thematic Review of Suicide Prevention

1.6 The review brings together the salient aspects of what is known about suicide risk and its assessment and management when expressed by people who present themselves to mental health-care services. The authors offer their opinions as to the current state of knowledge on clinical practice. Thus, much of the content will be of direct relevance to clinicians and managers in provider organisations. The text is, essentially, an aide-memoire for busy people.

1.7 Whilst much of the manual is slanted towards providers, there can be no doubt that it contains a wealth of information which is of direct relevance to those commissioning and specifying services and considering contract monitoring and quality assurance initiatives. Thus I hope that health authorities, family health service authorities and general practitioners (both fund-holding and non fund-holding) will find this text of direct relevance in dis-

charging their duties, generally, for ensuring the provision of comprehensive mental health services, and, specifically, for working towards achieving the Health of the Nation objectives and targets. They will find helpful information throughout but I have also included a specific chapter, Chapter 18, which draws out the general advice on principles of care for commissioners.

The Authors

1.8 I take this opportunity to record my gratitude to all those who have worked so hard on this Thematic Review.

1.9 Professor Gethin Morgan, who is the author of much of the document and my Research and Development Consultant, deserves particular gratitude. He and his team in the University of Bristol have gained vast experience in the field. Additionally, I know that Dr John Lambourn, Consultant Psychiatrist, Rose Jones, Principal Clinical Psychologist, and Joy Wilshire, Manager and Community Psychiatric Nurse, all of the South Devon Healthcare NHS Trust, Dr John Owen, Consultant Psychiatrist, Frenchay Healthcare NHS Trust, Dr Christine Johnson of the University of Bristol, Dr David Healey, Director of the Academic Sub-Unit of the University of Wales College of Medicine Department of Psychological Medicine, Dr S Fraser, Clinical Psychologist, Leicestershire Mental Health Services NHS Trust, and Mrs June Johnstone, Professor Morgan's indefatigable secretary, have provided him with invaluable support, information, and advice. Professor Morgan has devoted a considerable amount of his distinguished academic and clinical career to studying suicide prevention, particularly the assessment and management of those people who are at risk of killing themselves. The authority of his wisdom in this challenging arena of service philosophy, strategy, provision and practice, established internationally as well as within the UK, and his compassionate concern for people suffering the anguish of hopelessness and despair permeate this text.

1.10 The thanks of the HAS are also owed in large measure to the authors of the specialist chapters including those on adolescents and the implications for commissioners. The latter chapter was prepared by Mr Mike Farrar, Mental Health Strategy Manager at the Northern and Yorkshire Regional Health Authority Regional Office. His strategic wisdom and insights have already proved invaluable to the HAS in exercising its new roles, and the clarity of his thinking is demonstrated in this document. Chapter 11 – Adolescents – was prepared by a team of acknowledged experts in the field. I am indebted to Dr John Coleman, a health psychologist and Director of the Trust for the Study of Adolescence, for preparing the original text and acting

as the focal author in this part of the project. He has been assisted throughout by Professor Peter Hill, of St George's Hospital Medical School, and Professor Michael Kerfoot, Senior Lecturer and Director (Staff Development), Mental Health Social Work Research and Staff Development Unit in the University of Manchester. These three professionals of international repute have brought together their vast clinical and academic experience to provide this succinct review.

1.11 Finally, thanks are due to a force of others who have worked assiduously to ensure completion of this review. It includes Mrs Jenny Croft, who, as subeditor, has ensured that the text has been presented in an available and uniform style, and all the staff of the headquarters of the HAS.

Richard Williams

Director

NHS Health Advisory Service

July 1996

Chapter Two

A Guide to this Review

Aims

2.1 The recent publication of the Government White Paper, The Health of the Nation, challenges us all to address with renewed vigour the problems of suicide prevention. Health care professionals need to review thoroughly their clinical practice and underlying attitudes. The assessment and management of suicide risk is not an esoteric exercise; suicide can complicate a great variety of clinical situations. **Suicide is not always preventable, but sound clinical practice can help to avert it in certain clinical situations.**

2.2 Part A sets out some important and basic facts about suicide and Part B then proceeds to outline the various practical tasks involved in evaluating and managing suicide risk. Emphasis is placed upon a succinct identification of key points and the difficulties which may be encountered in their implementation. Such a brief text cannot pretend to be comprehensive, but it does concern itself with the most common and important issues involved, its priorities dictated by the realities of day-to-day clinical work. The clinical procedures that are discussed should not be considered in isolation, but as an integral part of a wider routine assessment involving first a full history, then systematic assessment of mental and physical states, followed by diagnostic categorisation. Only then can management be planned.

2.3 Part C is concerned with a number of vulnerable groups, including adolescents and young people. These groups have their own characteristics and present special challenges to those concerned with their care. Part D is aimed specifically at managers, although it is hoped that they will read the whole review, as only in this way will they be able to set the decisions that are before them in the context of good clinical practice.

2.4 The text presented here has drawn widely on the current literature in bringing together what is, in effect, a set of practical clinical guidelines. It is essentially a practical manual, not a substitute for text-book reading. References are given throughout the text so that the original literature can be accessed as the need arises.

2.5 Clinical guidelines in general have recently come under scrutiny.[1] This document is concerned with clinical guidelines in the sense that they are a general statement of principle, as opposed to protocols which cover the more detailed development of such basic principles for local application. At the present time, when psychiatric services are undergoing rapid change, it is crucial that the basic elements in the care of suicidal people should be debated fully to ensure that they are not compromised, whatever the clinical setting.

2.6 It should be emphasised early in this text that the guidelines set out here should not be taken to imply that there is only one, mandatory, way of undertaking the clinical tasks which are dis-

[1] Delamothe, 1993.

cussed; this would stifle initiative and prevent discretion in individual cases. Techniques other than those presented here may be both more imaginative and more effective. Indeed, clinical techniques will develop and evolve with time and it is hoped that the principles underlying matters considered in this text will contribute to these developments. Nevertheless, it is believed that the points made throughout the text are of fundamental importance in clinical care of suicidal people, and those who adopt alternative schemes may wish to consider them in the context of developing their own clinical procedures.

Using the Review

2.7   If it is to be effective in promoting best practice, it is important that this review is 'user-friendly'. While it is hoped that health care professionals, purchasers, managers, and those from the social services and from other agencies involved with mentally ill people will read the whole document, it is recognised that certain topics will be of greater interest than others to some readers. It is also hoped that readers will find it a handy reference text to consult on a specific point or to come back to for guidance. Every effort has

therefore been made to present the report in such a way as to make it easy to identify the section of particular interest. Each chapter is concerned with a specific topic and, for ease of reference, the original literature on which it draws is listed in footnotes in the chapters as well as in the comprehensive alphabetical bibliography at the end. There are also tables designed to present key information in a readily accessible form. The most important of these are brought together in the form of check-lists in Chapter 20 at the end. Some readers may find it helpful to abstract these in order to keep them to hand.

2.8   The review has also adopted the idea of 'key concepts'. These are printed in bold type as they occur in the text (see, for example, para 2.1 above) and are brought together at the end in Chapter 19. This approach is designed to highlight the crucial stages in the discussion and again help users identify quickly the portion of the text to which they wish to refer. They are not recommendations but, when brought together, represent a summary of our views on the essential elements underlying an effective strategy for suicide prevention.

PART A

BACKGROUND CONSIDERATIONS

Chapter Three

Some Facts and Figures

Numbers

3.1 Before discussing the clinical aspects of suicide prevention, it is essential to have the basic facts and figures in mind, in order to set the clinical task in context. All the statistics used in this Chapter are from OPCS Reports or from The Health of the Nation White Paper.

3.2 **Suicide is one of the major causes of death, accounting for 1% of all deaths annually.** In 1990, a total of 4,485 people killed themselves in England, Wales and Scotland. That is 86 people each week, 12 people every day, or one person every two hours. This represents an increase of 6% over the figure for 1989. Coroners vary in their criteria for recording a suicide verdict. Including the category of 'undetermined' deaths, that is deaths by injury where it cannot be ascertained whether that injury was accidentally or purposefully inflicted, reduces the variation considerably. Most undetermined deaths are suicide. **Thus, since it is likely that many suicides are recorded as 'undetermined' deaths, the suicide rate is probably even higher than it appears.**

3.3 **Suicides by men outnumber those by women by a ratio of more than 2:1.** In adolescents this rate is even higher at 5:1 (see Chapter 11). **The increasing suicide rates amongst young males give cause for concern, having increased by 75% in the 15-24 year old age group since 1982,** and merit separate consideration in this document –

but the highest suicide rates are still found amongst elderly people, in particular those aged over 75. In 1989 the rate per million for this group was 43% higher than the average. The suicide rate is particularly high in April, May and June. It is important to understand the age/sex specific rates of suicide, because the various population sub-groups differ considerably with regard to both rates and trends over time. For instance, recent increases in certain sub-groups of young adult women of Asian origin are worrying. There are also regional differences within the United Kingdom, as is illustrated in Table 2.

Table Two

Suicide Rates in the United Kingdom 1989

(Per 100,000 Population – Age 15 and Over)

	Males	Females
England and Wales	14	4
Scotland	19	7
Northern Ireland	21	5

Methods

3.4 In men, the use of car exhausts (32%), and hanging and suffocation (31%), are the two most common methods of suicide. In women, self-poisoning with solid substances (43%) accounts for the largest proportion of suicides, the commonest agents being analgesics, anti-pyretics, tranquillisers and other psychotropic drugs. Table 3 gives figures for the main methods of suicide in England and Wales in the period 1988-1990.

Table Three

Main Methods of Suicide: 1988 – 1990 (England and Wales)
(People aged 15 and over)

	Males	Females
	%	%
Car exhaust	32	11
Self-poisoning	15	43
Hanging	31	25
Firearms	5	1
Drowning	2.5	6

Correlates and Causes

3.5 In looking at correlates and causes of suicide, it is important to be clear that personal and social factors which may have a positive statistical association with suicide are not necessarily in themselves causal. Nevertheless, in clinical practice, care must be taken to evaluate whether or not they are present: the precise significance of each has to be determined in every individual, depending on the overall clinical assessment. There is a number of clinically useful socio-demographic and individual factors which are associated with increased risk of suicide:

- elderly
- male
- divorced>widowed>single
- unemployed or retired
- living alone (socially isolated)
- physical illness, especially terminal illness or painful or debilitating illness
- history of deliberate self-harm
- family history of affective (mood) disorder, alcoholism or suicide
- bereavement in childhood
- social classes I and V
- psychiatric and personality disorders

3.6 Taking up the last point from the list, it is important to note that when representative samples of people who have committed suicide have been examined utilising 'psychological autopsy', a method which consists of interviewing relatives and friends of deceased persons as well as scrutinising medical records, over 90% have been judged to have some form of psychiatric illness[1,2]. In those few suicides which lack evidence of such illness, it may nevertheless have been present, but undetected because of the unreliability of retrospective analysis. So-called 'rational' suicide, that is, suicide in the absence of manifest psychological distress, appears to be rare in Western countries.

Psychiatric Illness

3.7 All categories of psychiatric illness carry an increased risk of suicide. The following list ranks the various diagnostic groups in decreasing order of risk:

1. Depression (all forms).
2. Schizophrenia.
3. Alcoholism.
4. Drug addiction.
5. Organic cerebral disorder (eg, epilepsy, brain injury, mild dementia).
6. Personality disorder (especially sociopathy, impulsivity, aggression, lability of mood).
7. Neuroses.

3.8 Within high-risk diagnostic categories, attempts have been made to identify specific clinical features associated with increased risk. These are illustrated in Table 4.

[1] Barraclough et al, 1974.
[2] Rich et al, 1986.

Table Four

Suicide and Psychiatric Disorders: high risk factors within high risk diagnoses

Diagnosis	Risk Factors
Depression (Lifetime risk of suicide = 15%)[3]	Male, older Persistent insomnia Previous act of deliberate self-harm Self-neglect Severe illness Impaired memory Agitation Panic attacks
Schizophrenia (Lifetime risk of suicide = 10%)[3]	Male Younger Unemployed Previous act of deliberate self-harm Depressive episodes Anorexia/weight loss More serious illness Recurrent relapse Fear of deterioration, especially in those of high intellectual ability
Alcohol addiction (Lifetime risk of suicide = 3.4%)[4]	Male (peak age 40-60 years old) High level of dependency Long history of drinking Disruption of major interpersonal relationships Depressed mood Poor physical health Poor work record in previous four years

Social Factors

3.9 Isolation, estrangement or alienation from others are important social correlates of suicide, as are adverse life events, particularly in the form of losses of various kinds. Bereavement features prominently, especially in elderly people. Unemployment has been a recent focus of concern. Whilst poverty in itself does not correlate with suicide risk, loss of possessions or status does: events leading to a sense of humiliation are also significant. Suicide rates are highest in the upper and lowest social classes, the lowest rates occurring in skilled artisans. Other social influences include the role of imitation which may underlie 'suicide epidemics' in hospital,

and in closed communities such as religious groups in which there is intense shared belief, especially when outside events are perceived as threatening.

3.10 As a result of failure to respond to help – perhaps after recurrent relapse or because of challenging behaviour – not uncommonly people who proceed to commit suicide become severely and progressively distanced and alienated from those around them during the period immediately before they die. This has been termed[5] 'malignant alienation'. Recurrent depression is particularly liable to produce a negative, judgemental response after repeated relapse, and such alienation can contribute to the final state of total despair.

Occupational Groups at Special Risk

3.11 Concern has focused on recent increases in suicide rates in farmers (including horticulturalists, farm managers and male farm workers) where the rates are $1\frac{1}{2}$ to 2 times those expected in the general population. This may be associated with the social isolation often found in rural life, though ease of access to firearms and toxic agents is also relevant. There are also other occupational groups at increased risk; these include doctors, veterinary surgeons, pharmacists and dentists.

Risks Associated with Non-Fatal Deliberate Self-Harm

3.12 Persons who have deliberately, nonfatally harmed themselves (most commonly this involves some form of drug overdosage or self-laceration) are at greatly increased risk of committing suicide at some later date. Indeed a significant proportion of persons who do commit suicide have already made an

[3] Miles, 1977.
[4] Murphy & Wetzel, 1990.

[5] Watts & Morgan, 1994.

attempt to kill themselves at some time in the past. It has been shown[6] that such individuals, when followed up for ten years, have suicide rates which are 30 times those expected. In the year following deliberate self-harm (DSH), about 1% kill themselves, a rate which is 100 times that which is expected for the general population. The highest risk appears to be in the first three years, especially the first six months, following an overdose. Within the overall category of DSH patients there are established risk factors which correlate statistically with eventual suicide. These include male gender, social class V, unemployment, previous DSH, substance abuse and previous psychiatric history. It is worth noting that the problem of substance abuse (alcohol or drugs) has become of very great importance in recent years and brings with it the need for appropriate preventive strategies as well as effective, well co-ordinated, secondary care services.

3.13   The DSH group of patients is an important one, constituting the most common cause of emergency admissions to hospital medical wards for women, and in men second only to ischaemic heart disease. The incidence of DSH is greatest in younger adults, and more common in women than in men, though the male rates have risen in recent years so that the sex difference is now less marked than previously. In recognition of its importance and its distinctive characteristics, DSH is dealt with at some length in Chapter 14, and paragraphs 11.8 to 11.17 in Chapter 11 deal specifically with DSH in adolescents.

Access to Agents

3.14   The immediate availability of a means of suicide which is certain in action and preferably painless is an important factor in determining whether or not an individual will commit suicide. The change from toxic town gas in the 1960s probably helped avoid a considerable number of suicides. Someone who despaired at home could no longer act without reflection; if a visit to the chemist was necessary to buy the means of self-destruction, this might well have given time for ambivalent attitudes to help stave off the final act. While it is likely that some method substitution did occur, in spite of this the overall suicide rate still fell considerably in the 1960s. The recent emergence of motor-vehicle exhaust as a method of suicide, more evident in men, indicates an important theme in suicide prevention which needs serious consideration. It may be that the introduction of catalytic converters and stricter exhaust emission controls will have the same effect as the alteration in the composition of household gas in the 1960s. There is also convincing evidence from the USA concerning access to fire-arms which supports the hypothesis that easy availability of agents is an important factor in the genesis of suicide. In the UK, the high rates of suicide in farmers, doctors and other related practitioners may in part reflect ease of access to lethal agents such as firearms, drugs or poisons.

Further Reading on Suicide Statistics

3.15   The summarised text presented in this chapter is not intended to be an authoritative statement on suicide statistics. Its intention is to establish certain key matters for consideration. Readers who wish to pursue statistics on suicide further will find two excellent and up-to-date reviews on suicide available from HMSO. These should be consulted as sources of reference on matters such as rates, trends and analysis of causes (Charlton et al, 1992, 1993).

[6] Nordentoft et al, 1993.

Chapter Four

Negative Attitudes

4.1 The importance of having a positive attitude towards suicide prevention cannot be over-emphasised. However, a negative approach is all too common. Some people, including mental health professionals, sit on the fence as far as suicide prevention is concerned. When those people who are at risk of suicide seek professional help, they may already have talked to relatives and friends. The consultation, the contact with the professional, may well be the last port of call. They watch intently for a response. They are usually ambivalent about suicide and we have a responsibility to encourage the wish to live. We will fail in that task if we allow any lack of enthusiasm to influence attitudes towards providing help. In a professional approach, there is no room for value judgements on whether life is no longer worthwhile for the person contemplating suicide. Anyone who has extensive experience in suicide prevention will know that things can improve in a most unexpected way, even in the case of individuals facing what may seem enormous adverse odds. **It is vital to assume that such change for the better is always possible.**

4.2 Negative attitudes can take a variety of forms. Readers may find it a useful – and illuminating – exercise to test their own attitudes against those set out in Check-List 2 (page 103) which sets out commonly encountered negative views on the feasibility of suicide prevention. Negative attitudes tend to focus on a number of problems, both practical and philosophical, relating to how realistic any targets for suicide prevention are. Table 5 below sets out some of the commonest in the form of questions and, if not quite 'model answers', then appropriate responses. Paragraphs 4.3 to 4.6 provide a general, if less detailed, summation of those responses.

Table Five

Question	Response:
Should it not be left for each individual to decide about suicide?	Health care professionals are in a specially privileged position, very different from others. It is possible that a person at risk confronts the professional in order to sound out our attitude to suicide, as a last port of call. Whilst we should not aim to control others' lives when it may be inappropriate to do so, the well-recognised ambivalence of the suicidal person demands that we should attempt, whenever possible, to restore hope rather than confirm despair.
Not all suicides can be prevented: by focusing down on them, will we not merely accentuate the guilt feelings of health care professionals who did their best under difficult circumstances?	The targets merely enjoin us to attempt the prevention of the minority of suicides which might be preventable. It is fully accepted that some will still occur, despite excellent clinical care, and others will not even make contact with services.
Unless adverse political and social factors are dealt with, and these are not within the power of health care professionals to influence, what hope is there of reducing suicide rates?	While adverse conditions and events are undoubtedly important, nevertheless individual factors such as personal vulnerability and mental illness play a significant part in leading to suicide. In attempting to achieve a modest reduction in suicide rates, it seems sensible to look at ways of improving the mental health care of individuals at risk.

Table Five continued

Is it feasible to expect health care professionals to contribute to a reduction in suicide rates when suicide is such a rare event?	The incidence of suicide is very similar to that of 'common' organic diseases such as ulcerative colitis, Crohn's disease and multiple sclerosis. It has been argued that incidence figures are not a valid comparison as the prevalence of these organic disorders is considerably higher. However, this misconstrues suicide as a one-off episode, whereas it is, in fact, followed by a prolonged trail of emotional devastation in key others; the prevalence of this should be taken into account in measuring the total impact of suicide in our community. Strangely enough, we do not encounter reservations with regards to early detection and prevention of the organic illnesses cited above. So why the defeatist attitude about the task of suicide prevention? Suicide risk often extends over a long period of time before suicide finally occurs and can be encountered throughout most, if not the whole, diagnostic range of psychiatric disorders. The low base rate of suicide does mean that a GP with a practice size of 6,000 may encounter only once each year a patient who proceeds to commit suicide soon after consultation, though a group practice which serves a greater population would meet proportionately more. Some argue that it is not feasible to attempt the prevention of such a 'rare' event. But this is to construe suicide as akin to an exotic disease which appears only once in every four or five years, and which is not present at other times. This, of course, is far from the truth. Suicide risk in various forms and severities presents itself at practically every GP surgery, and if GPs were not skilled at responding to it, the incidence of suicide would be far greater than it is. The principles of care inherent in suicide prevention do indeed relate to the whole spectrum of clinical psychiatric practice from the assessment and management of depressed people to those who are personality disordered and exhibit challenging and aggressive impulsive behaviour. Each GP probably encounters each year ten patients who exhibit some form of non-fatal deliberate self-harm: among these, some will present significant suicide risk. If we improve these many facets of clinical care the suicide rates will probably themselves become reduced. To see the rates as an end in themselves is misjudged.
Surely persons who commit suicide do not seek help before the event; so what part can doctors be expected to play in preventing such deaths?	On the contrary, a significant number of people who commit suicide do seek medical help before they kill themselves. Thus a recent study[1] in Avon of unexpected deaths classified as suicide on clinical grounds has shown that 55% had seen their GP in the last three months of their lives and 26% had been in contact with mental health services. It was also demonstrated that young men who kill themselves, when compared with older suicides, are far less likely to seek such help either from medical or psychiatric services. It has to be conceded that this is a particularly worrying finding with regard to suicide prevention, because it is in young men, and in no other group, that significant and progressive increases in suicide rates have been demonstrated throughout England in recent years. The above rates of GP contacts apply to an urban area which has a significant city centre type of health problems. Other less urban areas may have much higher GP contact rates[2].
Even when suicidal individuals make contact they may come in clinical disguise. How can we be expected to see through these?	It is, of course, easy to be wise after the event, but to pick out those who will proceed to suicide from all others who consult us, can be a very difficult task. Yet by refining basic clinical procedures and with a thorough knowledge of risk factors we can, and should, be able to get better at it. In fact a considerable proportion of people at risk do talk openly about suicidal intent.
Surely it is dangerous to open up the topic of suicide with someone at risk?	This is a myth. Careful explanation and sharing of these ideas is itself preventative. (The relevant clinical skills are discussed later in Chapter 6).

[1] Vassilas & Morgan, 1993.

[2] Barraclough et al., 1974.

Sometimes a person's life situation becomes truly hopeless and impossible to face. In such circumstances, should not suicide be regarded as the best solution for that individual?

Even simple listening can help alleviate such despair. Many would claim that we should do all we can to prevent the extreme psychological distress of terminal despair.

Is it not true that once a person gets into a suicidal crisis, then suicide is inevitable?

The fact that individuals who commit suicide often 'shop around' for help before killing themselves suggests otherwise. The ambivalence of intent in suicidal persons is well recognised, and hope is usually retained to the very end of their lives. This argues against imperviousness to persuasion. Clinical experience with suicidal people demonstrates the immense value of reaching out and listening in helping to resolve a suicidal crisis, no matter how complex and apparently insoluble the individual's problems may seem to others.

Will attention be focused on the needs of men, especially young men, in whom increasing rates are causing concern, at the expense of women?

Co-ordinated planning should avoid this. Overall national statistics can be misleading as a guide to the identification of suicidal individuals. Those who plan clinical services must be mindful that suicide can occur in all age and gender groups and none of these should be ignored, even though increases in young adult men do cause concern. Much will depend on the specific population subgroups under consideration; for example, one study has shown that in psychiatric hospital suicides women under 40 numerically exceeded those in men[3].

Is it not hazardous to engage in formal reviews at a time when medical litigation is escalating?

Any audit procedure, or whatever other form of clinical review is undertaken, must pay full regard to concerns of this kind. It should be possible, however, to conduct clinical reviews in such a way that individual patients are not identified in any documentation.

Even when serious suicide risk is recognised, surely present-day clinical techniques in preventing such deaths are relatively ineffective and unlikely to influence the course of events?

This present manual spells out clinical techniques and their rationale.

4.3 It is sometimes felt that it is wrong to intervene and that it should be left for each individual to decide about suicide. Against this there is the well-recognised ambivalence of suicidal people which demands that, wherever possible, the attempt should be made to restore hope rather than confirm despair. Not all suicides can be prevented, despite excellent clinical care. Health care professionals should bear this in mind and not feel that by focusing on prevention they will accentuate feelings of guilt when they do not succeed. There is sometimes a feeling that it is not feasible to expect health care professionals to contribute to a reduction in suicide rates unless adverse factors which are outside their influence are also dealt with. However, while adverse conditions and events are important, individual factors such as personal vulnerability and mental ill-ness play a significant part in leading to suicide. Improving the mental health care of individuals at risk can undoubtedly contribute to some reduction in suicide rates.

4.4 Nor is the argument that suicide is a rare event an adequate reason for not focusing attention on its prevention. The incidence of suicide is very similar to that of what are often described as 'common' organic diseases such as ulcerative colitis. Suicide should not be seen as a one-off episode; it is followed by a prolonged trail of emotional devastation in others. The prevalence of this should be taken into account in measuring the total impact of suicide on the community. Suicide risk often extends over a long period of time before suicide finally occurs and can be encountered throughout most, if not the whole, diagnostic range of psychiatric disorders.

---

[3] Morgan and Priest, 1991.

The principles of care inherent in suicide prevention relate to the whole spectrum of clinical psychiatric and mental health service practice from the assessment and management of depressed people to those who are personality disordered and exhibit challenging and aggressive, impulsive behaviour.

4.5   It is sometimes argued that prevention is not possible because persons who commit suicide do not seek help before the event. This is not true; significant numbers of people who commit suicide do seek medical help before they kill themselves. A recent study[1] has shown that 55% of suicides had seen their GP in the last three months of their lives and 26% had been in contact with mental health services. Identifying those who proceed to commit suicide from others who seek help can be a very difficult task. However, by refining basic clinical procedures and with a thorough knowledge of risk factors, it should be possible to improve on present performance.

4.6   It is a myth that it is dangerous to open up the topic of suicide with someone at risk. A considerable proportion of people who commit suicide do talk openly about their suicidal intent. Careful explanation and sharing of ideas is itself preventative. Nor is it true that once a person gets into a suicidal crisis, suicide is inevitable. The fact that individuals who commit suicide often 'shop around' for help before killing themselves and their ambivalence about dying suggests otherwise. Clinical experience with suicidal people demonstrates the immense value of reaching out and listening in helping to resolve a suicidal crisis, no matter how complex and apparently insoluble the individual's problems may seem.

The Positive Approach

4.7   Not all negative attitudes to suicide prevention are deeply entrenched and immutable. A lecture which presented to health care professionals the basic facts about suicide, reviewed the principles of good clinical practice in the assessment and management of suicide risk and challenged negative attitudes (in the way this has been done in the present chapter), appeared to have a significant effect in reducing the degree of negativism towards the feasibility of suicide prevention.[4,5] Basic educational initiatives of this kind are essential components of any clinical service which aims to be effective in suicide prevention.

4.8   Underlying all that is said in the following chapters on the assessment and management of people at risk of suicide is the conviction that strategies for prevention will be most effective when they spring from a positive commitment. This commitment, **the belief that it is feasible to prevent at least some suicides, should permeate all those concerned with the treatment of a suicidal individual, whether in hospital or in the community.** Only in that way will the task be tackled with the thoroughness and comprehensive attention to detail that bring results.

---

[1] Vassilas & Morgan, 1993.
[4] Morgan & Evans, 1994.
[5] Morgan et al, 1994.

PART B

THE CLINICAL TASK

Chapter Five

Assessment of People at Risk of Suicide

Risk Factors – a Note of Caution

5.1 It would seem common sense, when faced with an individual who is suspected of being at risk of suicide, to search for demographic and clinical factors known to be associated with increased suicide risk. For example, a doctor, or other health care professional, assessing a patient in hospital following a non-fatal drug overdose would be particularly concerned if the patient was elderly, male, had suffered some kind of loss event recently, was socially isolated or alienated, had a family history of suicide and depressive illness, currently exhibited significant depressive symptoms, abused alcohol, had a chronic physical illness and a previous history of deliberate self-harm. This is the statistical stereotype of suicide. All these factors are well-known statistical correlates of suicide and must not be ignored. They do, however, present problems in the day-to-day clinical situation. Many individuals will possess these characteristics yet not commit suicide, and suicide can occur in people of very different characteristics. **Risk factors are correlates and associates, and not necessarily causes of suicide. They are more effective in predicting risk in the long-term rather than the immediate future.**

5.2 Prediction of suicide in the short-term, that is, over the next few hours or days, is an important routine clinical task. Whilst the judicious use of traditional statistical correlates has great value, **the final evaluation of risk must depend upon individual clinical assessment and that must take into account the differential weight-ings of risk factors in each person.** Particular care should also be taken to evaluate recent events and relationships, especially their intractability or ease of resolution, in building up a picture of short-term risk. It must always be remembered that suicide risk may be only one of several hazards relevant to any individual. For example, the concurrent risk of aggressive or violent behaviour should never be ignored. The relevant clinical techniques are not dealt with in the present text and should be sought elsewhere.

The Meaning of Suicidal Symptoms and Behaviour

5.3 The evaluation of suicide risk does not consist only of the detection of suicidal symptoms and their frequency or intensity. Suicidal ideation always has a complex meaning which can vary greatly in its significance of risk from one individual to another. **Suicide risk in any individual can only be assessed effectively by full clinical evaluation consisting of a thorough review of the history and present illness, assessment of mental state and then a diagnostic formulation.** To illustrate the task it is useful to consider two contrasting clinical stereotypes:

First:

This stereotype is of a person experiencing total despair with a final commitment to suicide. The patient may not admit to suicidal ideas or may actually deny them as a way of avoiding admission to hospital or accepting other forms of treatment and care or the interventions of other people: it may then be necessary to infer the presence of suicidal ideas from discrepancies between what the patient says and actual behaviour. There may be a history of severe life-endangering self-harm, either in the distant past or more recently, and the clinical picture may include severe psychological disturbance, such as the distorted insight of depressive illness, with self-blame and a sense of hopelessness, or other major psychiatric disorders.

Second:

The self-harm behaviour appears to be a function of the person's discontent with relationships, events or circumstances and in itself may have the appearance of being trivial, aimed primarily at influencing the response of other people. It seems to be a form of behaviour which is concerned mainly with delivering a message and which is designed to have an impact on others. There may be a long history of personality type difficulties, often with recurrent self-harm behaviour which has not been life-endangering. Although there may not be evidence of formal mental illness, such people often show extreme fluctuations in mood state, especially under the impact of stressful events or circumstances. They are often dismissed as merely using gestures and harmless threats of suicide: they become unpopular and run the risk of finally becoming very alienated from others.

5.4   In reality, most patients fall between these two extremes and their state may even fluctuate from one category to the other. In the first stereotype, the clinician may be the last port of call and his or her response, in trying to engender hope, is of fundamental importance. In the second stereotype it is important to remember that alienated, personality-disordered persons can respond positively to someone who is prepared to

listen to them, even though that person may not feel able to alter their life circumstances to any significant degree. Those dealing with persons who fall in the second category are sometimes inclined to insist that they should be treated as entirely responsible for their own destiny. While it may be necessary in certain cases to set very clear limits and strategies which require a degree of personal responsibility about how to behave (if only to avoid reinforcing maladaptive behaviour or excessive dependence on others), it is very important to realise that serious suicide risk may occur in both of the clinical stereotypes outlined above. Each individual requires careful clinical evaluation in order to establish the precise level of risk which, in any case, can fluctuate in severity from time to time. The assessment and management of suicide risk in personality-disordered persons is one of the most difficult of all clinical tasks.

The State of Mind of Suicidal Individuals

5.5   In reaching out to understand and assess the significance of suicidal symptoms and behaviour, it is helpful to have a picture in mind about what it really must be like to entertain serious ideas of ending one's life. Evidence suggests that ambivalence exists until a very late stage in the majority of those who proceed to kill themselves, and so, presumably, a debate occurs in the individual's mind as to whether or not suicide should be carried out. It follows that the clinician's reaction to that person, and positive attitudes concerning whether or not that life is worth preserving and the conviction that it is feasible to do so, may be of crucial importance in deciding which side will win the debate in the suicidal individual's mind.

5.6   A further important point concerns the role of impulse: it is likely that the easy availability of an effective method of self-destruction can be crucial at a time when hope fails and despair worsens. Yet despair is often a transient state, perhaps lasting for minutes or hours, often reflecting the impact of adverse day-to-day events. The technique of playing for time, and devising ways of defusing such crises, and identifying life-lines, can be of great importance in reducing the acute risk of suicide. Constriction of conceptual thinking into a dichotomy – seeing outcome as either death or one other, intolerable, option – also needs to be recognised and dealt with as part of any therapeutic response to suicide risk. The aim should be to get the individual to admit several possible alternatives to death as acceptable outcomes, even though they may all be less than perfect solutions to the crisis.

'Problem' Patients and Malignant Alienation

5.7   Difficult and unco-operative behaviour on the part of suicidal patients has long been documented.[1,2] It is wrong to equate suicide risk exclusively with the classic picture of severe depressive illness, important though this is: angry, unco-operative individuals may be just as much at risk. Many of these may have acquired the diagnostic label of personality disorder because of behavioural difficulties extending back over many years. This should **not** be taken to mean that they may never get into difficulties where suicide risk may be severe and require short-term crisis intervention in its own right, even including a compulsory procedure

under the Mental Health Act 1983, if necessary. In other words, persons who have personality disorders can at times develop depressive states severe enough to be categorised as depressive illness, which might need to be treated in its own right.

5.8   It is not uncommon for a suicidal individual who has failed to respond to intensive help, perhaps relapsing repeatedly or behaving in a challenging and unco-operative way, to suffer major loss of support and sympathy from others. Attitudes become critical and judgemental, resulting in the person being perceived in pejorative terms, such as manipulative or over-dependent. Such a terminal syndrome prior to suicide has been termed 'malignant alienation'. Whenever such a situation arises it is important that all those involved should meet as a group to review it as fully and objectively as possible. In this way, an attempt can be made to identify those individuals who are at real risk of suicide, whose difficult behaviour reflects severe despair and total failure – through illness – to cope with their problems, as opposed to deliberate misbehaviour which might have been avoided by self-control.[3]

5.9   Suicide is an uncommon event. **Assessment of risk must depend primarily upon a thorough and comprehensive evaluation of the total clinical picture in each case,** and this includes social and relationship factors such as social isolation, alienation, lack of support and adverse life events. However, in spite of their low specificity and sensitivity, particularly in the short-term, **risk factors can still represent an important element in routine clinical assess-**

---

[1] Seager and Flood, 1965.

[2] Morgan, 1979.

[3] Watts and Morgan, 1994.

ment. They are particularly useful as a 'double check', suggesting caution if risk is judged to be trivial yet risk factors are prominent.

Chapter Six

Interview Techniques

6.1 It is vital to feel confident about carrying out the task of assessing suicide risk. In order to do this, knowledge of the basic technique involved and the hazards to be negotiated is essential. A person who has suicidal ideas may be in two minds about sharing these with anyone else, particularly on first encounter. **Interview technique should aim to bridge the gap created by mistrust, despair and loss of hope that anything can change for the better.** Check-List 3 (page 104) provides a useful ready reminder of the key principles of good interview technique in these circumstances.

6.2 Interviewers should keep in mind that they may be the last port of call in the process whereby suicidal persons seek out others, perhaps readily declaring their wish to end their lives. The response of interviewers is, therefore, vital; ignoring basic clinical principles may confirm suicidal despair, as any ambivalence on the interviewer's part will soon be perceived. **To reach out and listen is itself the first major step in reducing the level of suicidal despair.**

6.3 It is useful to lead into the topic of suicidal ideas gradually. This reinforces the impression that the interviewer is sensitive to a distressed individual's feelings and makes it more likely that these can safely be shared with another person. In parallel with direct questioning about suicidal ideas, circumstantial information is also important. Thus leaving a note, making a will, or other evidence of suicidal intent should be taken seriously. Discrepancies between behaviour and verbal reassurances should be seen as a reason for caution.

6.4 A useful sequence of questions is illustrated in Table 6. (It is also reproduced in Chapter 20 as Check-List 4, page 105). It should be noted that the process does not end with confirmation that suicidal ideas are present. It then continues with further questions aimed at determining their persistence and the degree to which they might be acted upon, as well as the risk to others, particularly close family members. Finally, it should lead on to ways of providing help.

Table Six

A Sequence of Questions Useful in Assessing Suicide Risk

These questions are designed to help discover whether the patient:

a. Hopes that things will turn out well.
b. Gets pleasure out of life.
c. Feels hopeful from day to day.
d. Feels able to face each day.
e. Sees a point in it all.
f. Ever despairs about things.
g. Feels that it is impossible to face the next day.
h. Feels life to be a burden.
i. Wishes it would all end.
j. Knows why he or she feels this way (eg wants to be with a dead person, life is bleak, morbid guilt).
k. Has thoughts of ending life; if so, how persistently?
l. Has thoughts about the possible method of suicide (is means readily available?).
m. Has ever acted on any suicidal thoughts or intentions.
n. Feels able to resist any suicidal thoughts or intentions; and has any thoughts about what would make them disappear.

The interviewer must then consider:

a. How likely the individual is to kill self.
b. The ability of the individual to give reassurance about safety (eg until next appointment).
c. The circumstances likely to make things worse.
d. The willingness of the individual to turn for help if a crisis occurs.
e. Risks to others.

6.5 In presenting this sequence, it is important to emphasise that the recommended procedure does not amount to a fixed list which should be followed in an interrogational way. While some might see questions as 'leading', almost suggesting to the patient that suicidal ideas are present, this is not the intention: to minimise this, it is perhaps wise to present each question in an open way, using polar opposites.

6.6 The process involves a real challenge in clinical assessment. The situation has to be created whereby the patient feels able to share suicidal ideas with another person, and overcomes any reluctance to do so. This should be achieved by the interviewer's attitude of concern and empathy, rather than any element of coercive questioning. To listen in an appropriate way is the first effective step in reducing suicide risk. It is a process of sharing and the patient may show overt evidence of relief during the interview. An aggressive style of questioning should always be avoided, no matter how challenging the behaviour of the patient. In particular, impulsive personality-disordered individuals, or those who are severely depressed and morbidly guilt-ridden, can be placed at increased risk by inappropriate interviewing technique.[1]

Difficulties in Assessing the Individual Patient

6.7 It is important to interview relatives and key others whenever possible to ascertain whether the person at risk has expressed suicidal ideas or posed a risk in any other way. Only by assessing evidence from a variety of sources can the degree of risk be evaluated correctly. The fluctuation of degree of suicidal intent and distress in suicidal individuals, often from one hour to the next, should also be borne in mind; the interviewer should recognise that individual clinical interviews can give a grossly misleading impression of the overall severity of suicide risk. Sometimes also, hospital patients experience major relief from distress on their removal from upsetting events, only to relapse rapidly if brought into contact with them once again. Misleading false improvement, merely through removal from stressful events, is a real hazard[2]. It should also be borne in mind that individuals deeply intent on killing themselves may deliberately deny such ideas as a way of deceiving the interviewer. Or, having made their decision, they may lose all objective signs of distress and appear calm, thereby giving a false appearance of being better. Check-List 5 (page 106) brings together some of the difficulties to be borne in mind in the assessment of those at risk of suicide.

[1] Goh et al, 1989.
[2] Morgan & Priest, 1991.

Chapter Seven

General Principles of Management of Suicide Risk and the Management of People at Risk of Suicide in the Community

Some Important General Points on Management

7.1   Practical procedures concerning day-to-day management of risk will vary according to the setting, particularly whether the patient remains in the community or is admitted to hospital. This chapter and the one following deal with care in the community and in the hospital respectively, but before turning to matters of detail, there are some important general issues affecting the individual's treatment, wherever it takes place, which must be addressed.

7.2   It needs to be emphasised at this juncture that the text presented here and in subsequent chapters does not attempt to establish a set of rigid mandatory clinical rules which merely stifle initiative. Clinical techniques will develop and evolve with time. Here are set out principles which it is hoped will contribute to and, possibly, guide such developments.

7.3   The comprehensive treatment of a person at risk of suicide depends upon the diagnosis and underlying causes which should initially be established by full clinical assessment involving a thorough history and mental state evaluation. Physical examination is an important component which should not be ignored, particularly in high risk groups such as elderly people. However, certain basic principles of care apply whatever the underlying

cause of the suicide risk. **Treatment begins when contact is made, preferably by procedures which reach out to persons at risk and encourage them to seek help at an early stage.** The image and face validity of the service offered is important, as is the principle of listening which should underpin the whole process of care. This is one of the most potent of techniques in resolving suicidal crises: giving time, acceptance, sympathetic understanding, quiet confidence and optimism are all components of this most important technique. Recognising its value strengthens therapists in their resolve in the face of situations which, otherwise, too easily are dismissed as beyond help.

7.4   Apart from the need to treat any specific disorder, whether organic or psychiatric, which may be present, there are certain basic therapeutic issues common to all cases of suicide risk. In describing what is involved, one can do no better than to quote from the doyen of suicidology, Edwin Shneidman[1]:

"Doing anything and almost everything possible to cater to the 'infantile' idiosyncrasies, the dependency needs, the sense of pressure and futility, the feeling of hopelessness and helplessness that the individual is experiencing. In order to help the highly lethal person one should involve others; create activity around the person; do what he or she wants done – and if that cannot be

---

[1] Shneidman, E, 1993.

accomplished at least move in the direction of the desired goals to some substitute goals, that approximate to those which have been lost".

and again:

"The main point of work with a lethally oriented person – in the give and take of talk, the advice, the interpretations, the listening – is to increase that individual's psychological sense of possible choice and sense of being emotionally supported. Relatives, friends, and colleagues should, after they are assessed to be on the life-side of the individual's ambivalence, be closely involved in the treatment process. Suicide prevention is not best done as a solo practice. A combination of consultation, and ancillary therapists, and the use of all the interpersonal and community resources that one can involve is, in general, the best way of proceeding".

These extracts emphasise the need for a thorough knowledge of the individual's strengths and vulnerabilities, so that the crisis is seen from that person's unique point of view. This is the approach that should inform treatment, whatever its setting.

Management in the Community

7.5 Clear communication, mutual support and sharing of skills are essential for all psychiatric care, but play a particularly important role in community settings. Agencies and services vary considerably, from a well-staffed psychiatric crisis intervention service to an isolated, single-handed GP. **The basis of good practice, wherever it is based, is the formation of a supportive understanding relationship with the patient.**

7.6 There are advantages to community care for less determinedly suicidal individuals. With support, he or she can use and improve coping skills to deal with stressors in a normal environment, as opposed to 'escaping' from problems, which can occur as a result of hospitalisation. The patient may well prefer community care which is seen as less stigmatising and less liable to reduce self-esteem, both of which can be problems arising from hospital inpatient treatment. Nor does the patient lose contact with family and usual carers, and with a normal environment. In short, patients retain their usual lifestyle, autonomy and responsibilities. It can also make matters easier for the therapist who will usually have easier access to relevant family dynamics and other contributing stressors which can then be addressed more directly.

7.7 There are, however, also some disadvantages. It may be more difficult to ensure safety in terms of close supportive care and a safe environment. There can be problems in relation to treatment compliance and in monitoring physical and medical conditions. The patient may be exposed to intolerable family tension, social isolation or hostility: hospital can provide a sanctuary from such stressors. The burden of care and the strain placed on family and carers should also be borne in mind when deciding on a community-based approach.

7.8 **Community management is not appropriate when suicide risk escalates beyond a critical level and there are significant limits in supporting mechanisms.** In lesser degrees of suicidal intent, community management is of great value. Increasing numbers of psychiatric patients are now being managed in non-hospital settings. The reduction of hospital facilities can mean that individuals at risk of suicide find themselves having to cope in the community, without the structured milieu and physical security of the hospital. Equally, community services are having to cope, perhaps for the first time, with patients who would previously have been managed in hospital. The aim of the following guidelines is to concentrate on the general principles of good community care and to identify important issues that should be borne in mind when working outside the hospital environment.

Deciding on Community Care

7.9 There is always a balance to be struck between the advantages and limitations of community care (see Table 7 below, also reproduced in Chapter 20, page 113 as Check-List 10). **Management in the community is appropriate where the suicidal intent of the person is judged to be manageable in that setting and there is good rapport with the patient.**

A significant history of impulsive behaviour, including serious acts of deliberate self harm (DSH), should be evaluated with particular care. Alcohol or drug intake, if relevant, should ideally be under adequate control, the patient should be compliant with the management plan, perhaps having agreed a treatment contract (see para 7.13 below) or have given a commitment not to harm him or herself.

If major stressors in the home setting are tolerable, the patient has skills in independent living, adequate housing and financial resources, and there are no physical complications, then there is much to be said in favour of the community approach, especially when it is the patient's preference.

Table Seven

Advantages and limitations of community care

Advantages

• With support from the therapist, the patient can use and improve coping skills to deal with relevant stressors in a normal environment (as opposed to escaping from stressors which may occur as a result of hospitalisation).

• The patient may prefer it: he or she may suffer less stigmatisation and less reduction in self-esteem – both of which can be problems arising from hospitalisation.

• The patient does not lose contact with his or her family, usual carers and normal invironment.

• The patient retains his or her usual life-style, autonomy and responsibilities.

• The therapist generally has easier access to relevant family dynamics and other contributing stressors which can then be addressed more directly.

Limitations

• It is more difficult to ensure safety in terms of close supportive care and safe environment.

• It is more difficult to ensure treatment compliance.

• It is more difficult to monitor physical and medical condition.

• It is more difficult to provide sanctuary from stressors (eg, patient may be exposed to intolerable family tension, social isolation or hostility).

• Family or carers may be placed under undue strain/burden of care or may be perceived to be so by the patient.

7.10 Before a final decision is made, however, a number of factors relating to the therapist who will be dealing with the patient in the community need to be considered. He or she should have had adequate training and feel confident in dealing with psychological problems. He or she must be prepared to allocate – and have – sufficient time to allow regular and flexible contact. There should be back-up available to provide support when the key therapist is not available. The appropriate prescription of medication in terms of amount of drug prescribed and how frequently should also be considered. Check-List 11 (page 114) provides a ready reference to all the factors, whether relating to the patient or the therapist, which must be considered before a decision on community management is taken.

Initial Assessment

7.11 Implicit in a decision to manage a patient in the community is the principle that the person retains the greatest possible responsibility for his or her own actions. Such a decision requires a good understanding of the patient. Emphasis must be placed on engaging the patient and gaining mutual trust and rapport. Adequate time should be allowed so that a full clinical history and examination can be carried out and careful consideration given to the factors set out above. Thorough initial assessment of psychological, social and physical aspects are essential, as these cannot be as easily monitored in the community as in a ward situation. A history should also be obtained from all relevant informants, in particular people who will be with the patient at home or have contact on a regular basis. Previous medical and psychiatric records should be sought out and referred to.

7.12 A home visit can be extremely useful as it can give a full picture of the patient's environment and the stressors to which he or she is being subjected, including family dynamics. An idea of the patient's values and level of social functioning or recent changes in these can also be obtained. A further advantage of a home visit is that potential dangers can be reviewed. For example, a large store of pills or a weapon can, with the patient's permission, be taken away during the vulnerable period. If such permission is not given, it may be that risk is greater than otherwise suspected and the possibility of admission to hospital should be considered very seriously. Local situational factors, such as a railway line or busy motorway adja-

cent to the home, or living in high-rise accommodation may influence the decision as to the appropriateness of community care, particularly when the individual expresses specific intent relating to them. Evidence of alcohol abuse should also be sought, even when this is specifically denied during interview.

7.13 Points which suggest caution in the assessment and management of patients in the community are brought together in Check-List 12 (page 115). **Grounds for caution should prompt a review of management** and perhaps the adoption of a more intensive form of care.

Setting up a Contract with the Patient

7.14 A written contract negotiated between the therapist and a suicidal patient can be a useful technique in suicide prevention. For many patients, a signed document can be a powerful symbol of commitment both to continue to live as well as to work at particular problems. Such a document can also make both the therapist and patient feel more secure, perhaps alleviating despair, and the act of negotiation of the contract can promote discussion of relevant issues. 'Contracting' is appropriate only when the patient has adequate control over his or her actions; it is particularly useful in a community setting. Other involved parties, such as family members, can be involved in negotiating a contract. Whilst refusal to sign a contract may stem from suicidal intent, it should be remembered that some patients refuse to collaborate with it as a matter of principle, irrespective of suicidal ideation. Such individual choice should be respected. Two copies of the contract should be made so that both parties can retain a copy. It should always include:

- **The date the contract was agreed**
- **The period of the contract**
- **A review date**

  The patient should be asked for how long he or she feels safe to give a commitment. This empowers the patient, giving him or her the choice and may also give an idea of how vulnerable he or she is feeling.

- **The patient's commitment**

  This usually includes not harming him or herself and not harming others, plus other appropriate commitments such as compliance with treatment.

- **The therapist's commitment**

  This should be determined in the light of the patient's specific needs. These may include frequency of contact and issues to be addressed.

- **A 'default clause'**

  This is a useful addition so that the patient has an alternative if he or she becomes acutely suicidal during the period of the contract; for example, if the patient feels unable to keep to his or her part of the contract, he or she agrees to contact his or her doctor to discuss changing or cancelling the contract.

- **Consequences of breaking the contract**

  These should be clearly stated. Inability to honour the contract must not be seen as a failure (which could lead to further self-blame) on the part of the patient. Great care should be taken to cover this issue in setting up the contract.

- **Signatures**

  Both parties should sign both copies of the document.

Continuing Care

7.15 Check-List 13 (page 116) sets out the tasks for the therapist once a decision on community management has been made. That review and evaluation of

suicide risk should include full systematic assessment of mental state, not just a casual and incomplete enquiry which can miss key clinical features. As with all psychiatric management, documentation and communications should be thorough during the whole period of care. A regular review of the patient's mental state and management plan should be made. The general approach should be supportive and flexible. Frequency of contact will vary depending on the needs of the individual patient and carers, but, initially, the number of contacts should err on the side of more rather than less, at least until an adequate therapeutic relationship has been established. This can mean more than one contact per day at first. Telephone contact is a possible adjunct, but should not be seen as equivalent to face-to-face contact.

7.16 An important component in efficient management is the mobilisation and co-ordination of community support. Professional agencies, voluntary groups, friends and relatives all have a helpful part to play in supporting a patient through his or her difficulties. In particular, the Samaritans can play an important role in suicide prevention in the community. This organisation has the advantage of being able to offer 24-hour a day availability and can provide time and support for despairing individuals, especially in times of crisis. As it is non-professional, the Samaritans can be perceived by some patients as more approachable than are doctors or allied professions. However, consistency of aim and approach is essential to ensure that a variety of support is not counter-productive. Case conferences or joint meetings are often very helpful; they should, however, always have a clear agenda.

7.17 During each contact with the patient, the time and place of the next appointment should be agreed. It is advisable to leave a contact number for the patient and carers. Advice and support may then be obtained between visits, if problems arise. Particular care should be taken to ensure that appropriate help can be acquired at weekends and on Bank Holidays if necessary. A problem-orientated approach (see Chapter 9) is often useful, but if tasks are given to the patient between contacts, it is important not to set up failures which may have harmful effects on the patient's self-esteem. Exploring with the patient the consequences of not attaining a particular goal may help minimise this risk.

7.18 Support and advice may well be required to ease the burden on family and carers and these should always be readily available. If difficulties in the home situation become too great, respite or sanctuary may be required. In addition to hospitalisation, alternatives such as moving to the home of a friend or relative, or other temporary accommodation, should be considered as these can, in certain circumstances, be more appropriate.

7.19 Any prescribing of medication should be in adequate therapeutic doses but prescribed in non-dangerous quantities. The reasons for prescribing should be discussed fully with the patient. In making the choice, the danger of medication, and its dangerousness in overdose, should be considered, as well as efficacy. The patient should be warned of potential side-effects and these should be monitored carefully. Sometimes it might be advisable, with the patient's agreement, to ask a responsible friend or relative to take charge of the prescribed medication for a while during times of increased risk.

7.20 Sometimes it may be necessary to provide long-term support for someone who continues to present a degree of suicide risk which does not resolve completely as a result of the fullest possible care. In such circumstances, regular supportive appointments can still be of great help, perhaps until some crucial change in the life-situation permits further progress to be made. If admission to hospital is considered, it is important to address any anxieties which the patient may have about this. Many individuals fear loss of control on being admitted to hospital. Everything should be done to reassure them, and indeed ensure in reality, that such will not be the case, and that members of the community team will maintain contact during any in-patient admission. Such continuity is of enormous value.

Appropriate Levels of Help

7.21 It is essential for the therapist to be clear about the level of help available and the ways of seeking more intensive review and assessment of the patient's clinical status, if cause for concern about suicide risk arises. There are various options, such as seeing the patient more frequently or consolidating support from relatives and other key persons. It may be necessary to contact colleagues for advice or to consult the mental health team as a whole. Special indications for consultation with the general practitioner or relevant psychiatrist should be clearly agreed. Finally, there is always the option of admission to hospital.

7.22 Quite often one member of the team dealing with a patient will want to discuss the situation with other members of a multidisciplinary team. The agenda for such discussions will vary according to the nature of the precise clinical problem and the good judgement of the practitioners concerned. It is important to focus on short-term risk and how the situation can be made as safe as possible. The schema in Table 8 below may be helpful. Any such discussion on the level of suicide risk and its immediate management should seek to answer two basic questions, namely whether the patient has had suicidal ideas in the recent past and whether those in contact are reassured that the patient is unlikely to act on those ideas. The answers to these questions should always be accompanied by the reasons for the view taken.

Table Eight

Points to cover in discussing level of suicide risk and its immediate management in the community.

1.

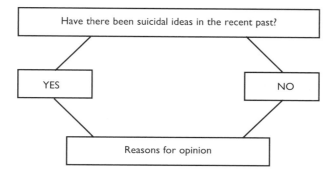

2.

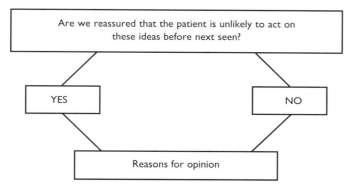

3.

What plan is proposed until the next appointment if the patient is to stay in the community?

- type of support.
- how often see the patient.
- support required and available from relations and other key persons.
- plan to be discussed with, and agreed by, patient and others.
- possible crisis times and what to do in crisis.
- telephone numbers to get help:
  a.   for patient
  b.   for therapist or others.
- access to medication (quantities safe, key others as caretakers, possible stores at home).

7.23 If the patient is to remain in the community then ideally the principles of the Care Programme Approach should be followed, although resource limitations at present do not always permit their full implementation in all patients. The Care Programme Approach ensures that a key worker is identified, with the responsibility of maintaining contact with the patient and co-ordinating the whole treatment plan by calling regular review meetings of all involved in the patient's care. Plans should be discussed with, and agreed by, the patient and others. The advent of supervision registers means that, according to initial advice,[2] patients who present a significant ongoing suicide risk would need to be included in those notified and monitored in this way. Possible risk times should be identified and action to be taken at such times discussed. The patient should be given telephone numbers to get help at times of crisis. Access to medication needs to be considered; for example, the quantity that is safe and the necessity of some other person having control of it. It may also be necessary to check the stores of medication at the patient's home if there is thought to be a risk of overdose.

Compulsory Hospital Admissions

7.24 The most difficult decisions concern patients who seem to be at severe and immediate risk of suicide, yet who are unwilling to accept any form of help: in such circumstances it may be necessary to arrange an immediate evaluation with a view to compulsory admission under one of the provisions of the Mental Health Act 1983. This is a major step and implies that the patient is no longer able to make responsible and safe decisions regarding personal safety and perhaps the safety of others.

The whole procedure is a matter of very careful judgement because a suicidal individual who is forced into hospital may find it so distressing that, at any subsequent relapse, he or she becomes unwilling to seek any help at all. This would be a severe price to pay for gaining an element of immediate safety. However, many suicidal individuals who are treated in hospital in this way subsequently express gratitude for the fact that other people felt obliged to take decisions, and indeed take over management from them at a time of very great risk. Such a possible outcome depends not only on the sensitivity with which the initial assessment is carried out, but also on the experience in the hospital ward itself, and the quality of care and facilities available there.

Discharge From Specialist Care

7.25 Whilst individuals may continue to have contact with health and other services for an indefinite period, those who are to be discharged from care need to have the planning for that discharge carried out with particular care. The discharge time should be negotiated with the patient and adequate time allowed so that the patient can work through the termination process of the therapeutic relationship. Exploration of how the patient will feel and cope beyond this termination is important. A gradual reduction in frequency of contact with the patient is preferable to a sudden cessation after intense involvement. Any unresolved stresses should be treated with great caution. If the patient is being referred on to a new service a gradual transition is most effective, allowing staff to be introduced to the patient before he or she is discharged from the present one, as well as for discussion between the two teams.

---

[2] Department of Health, 1994.

Chapter Eight

Management of People at Risk of Suicide in Hospital

8.1 Both absolute numbers and rates of suicide in psychiatric inpatients have increased progressively in several European countries during the last three decades. The precise reasons are not clear. Possible explanations include the greater proportion of short-term admissions of persons who are acutely ill, and changes in clinical practice. Whatever the explanation, **suicide in psychiatric hospitals has become an important clinical problem which demands careful evaluation of present-day clinical practice.**

8.2 The period soon after admission to hospital is well-recognised as a danger time for serious self-harm and suicide. Some of the explanations for this are obvious: the patient may not be well-known to members of staff, and the process of hospital admission can be a crisis in itself. Less obvious are the possible adverse side-effects of medication, particularly the inadvertent induction of unpleasant subjective tension and agitation. Great care should be taken in the case of patients who are already tense and impulsive, especially if clinical assessment suggests that suicide risk is present, so that their responses to medication are monitored very carefully.

The Admission Procedure and Assessment on Admission

8.3 Thorough, well-documented clinical assessment based on a clinical history and examination are the mainstay of good clinical practice in the care of suicidal people. The advantages of obtaining notes from another service which has cared for the patient previously,

and interviewing other informants, are obvious. The use of specialised risk questionnaires (see Chapter 10) can be a useful back-up to full clinical assessment but no more than that.

8.4 On accepting the referral of a suicidal person to hospital, the admitting doctor needs to obtain as much background information as is available from the referrer and other appropriate informants. Prior to the patient's appearance on the ward, the admitting doctor should communicate fully and directly with the ward nursing staff as to the possible risks. If there is to be any delay between the patient's arrival on the ward and the medical admission procedure, a clear decision should be made by the admitting doctor, after consultation with the nurse who is currently in charge of the ward, as to the required level of nursing observation during this period.

8.5 It is useful in some circumstances to ensure that during this critical period prior to admission assessment, persons at risk of suicide are kept in bed and nursed in pyjamas. When risk is judged to be significant and such precautions are thought necessary:
- all belongings that might pose a risk (eg ties and belts) should be removed;
- it should be possible to ensure that the patient remains visible to staff at all times and should not be allowed to leave the ward;
- caution should be employed in allowing cigarettes and matches;
- commode toilet facilities should be used at the bedside.

A clear decision should be made as to the degree of privacy that the patient is allowed, for example, whether at night curtains may be drawn around the patient's bed. Such precautions underline the many uncertainties which surround this period of care. All actions by the staff and their reasons need to be clearly communicated to the patient in a caring and supportive manner.

8.6 A full clinical history and examination should be carried out by the ward doctor as soon as possible following the arrival of the patient at hospital. This should include both mental state and a physical examination. In particular, a thorough review of suicidal intent, present difficulties and history of deliberate self-harm should be carried out. It is very helpful to interview, or perhaps consult by telephone, other relevant informants at the earliest opportunity, and previous casenotes can contain very useful data. Relevant information should be clearly documented and communicated to ward staff.

8.7 A treatment plan and appropriate levels of observation, agreed jointly by the doctor and nursing staff, need to be communicated to ward staff and the patient (as well as the patient's family and carers if appropriate). This, too, should be documented. Every effort should be made to keep key others informed as treatment proceeds. Again, great care is needed in the choice of medication, if this is to be used, especially when the patient exhibits agitated, impulsive behaviour which might be accentuated by any unwanted side-effects of drugs prescribed.

Ward Milieu

8.8 The facilities of the ward to which suicidal people are admitted need to be adequate in terms of physical safety, with reasonable control of well-recog-

nised hazards such as high windows and staircases. Sufficient security requires an appropriate control of ward exits and the identification of an area of the ward which allows complete control of access and exit for any patients requiring intensive supervision. **A guaranteed, minimum, agreed level of staffing is essential.** If any ward cannot meet the needs of high-risk individuals, then one which can provide more intensive care should be available, to which patients can be transferred as necessary. Ideally, extra staff should be made available, thereby avoiding the disruption which results from moving from one ward to another. A locked ward is now used very infrequently, because in normal circumstances, **intensive levels of supervision should depend on the appropriate provision of staff, rather than impersonal physical barriers.** Environmental hazards vary in significance from one individual to another; for example, an inflammable nightdress can present particular risk for a patient who has a preoccupation with setting fire to herself, especially if there is a history of doing so in the past. Seclusion areas within the ward need to be evaluated carefully, for example whether toilets should be lockable from the inside. Curtain rails in areas which set out to provide intensive care should permit only light weight-bearing. Windows should be secure where necessary.

8.9 Any ward offering care for acutely ill people is bound to experience disturbance from time to time. Suicide prevention requires a positive atmosphere in which clinical crises are dealt with as rapidly as possible, in a quiet, efficient way with the least possible disturbance to other patients. Wards that are too large make it difficult to deliver personalised care for individuals. Insufficient numbers of beds mean that the atmosphere becomes unsatisfactory, because of the need to move patients, which sometimes involves lodging them on other wards with little warning, and inevitably leads to a greater proportion of individuals becoming upset and exhibiting disturbed behaviour.

8.10 High patient morale depends upon adequate provision of basic facilities and good communications, not only between patient and therapist on an individual basis, but also within the ward community as a whole. This may be achieved in a variety of ways including ward meetings. Any interruption of normal routine, for example on Bank Holidays, represents an extra hazard for suicidal people, especially if ward rounds and other staff meetings are cancelled.

8.11 Nurses are in contact with patients for many hours of the day: they can play an important role in suicide prevention, not only because of their professional skills and experience, but also as a result of the morale which should permeate their work. In turn this depends upon regular availability of appropriate numbers of qualified staff. Unless staffing levels are satisfactory, the delivery of care to special-need groups, such as those who are suicidal, remains rudimentary. It is important to maintain an adequate nursing presence in the ward itself, especially during staff meetings and at the times of shift change-over.

8.12 The level of mutual trust that exists between the various professional groups, notably nurses and doctors, is very important and each must maintain respect for the other. When faced with patients who exhibit difficult behaviour, that trust can be strained. A situation akin to rivalry can develop as to who has the right to make decisions or countermand them. This does nothing for suicide prevention yet is, regrettably, more common than most practitioners might care to acknowledge. Team work is of paramount importance; the identification of a key worker to co-ordinate everybody's efforts can be an invaluable way of helping to establish an effective alliance with the patient who should be in no doubt about whom to contact for immediate advice and support at any time. The Care Programme Approach should be adopted whenever it is feasible and appropriate to do so.

Supportive Observation

8.13 The levels of supportive observation described below (paras 8.20 to 8.27) are designed to produce a consistency of approach when managing hospitalised suicidal patients, as well as to clarify terminology. They are based on the principle that intensity of care is matched to the degree of risk. Phrases which have ambiguous meanings for health care professionals such as 'special observation' or 'close observation' have been avoided in order to make communication more reliable and application more consistent.

8.14 **The appropriate level of supportive observation should be decided as a result of discussion between medical and nursing staff.** The agreed level, together with any risks and specific instructions, should be recorded in the medical and nursing notes of the patient concerned. Ideally it should be reviewed at every shift change of nursing staff and confirmed with the patient's doctor daily as well as being reviewed at the weekly ward round with the relevant senior staff. **Normally, the level of supportive observation should not be relaxed without joint medical and nursing consultation. It may be intensified,** if judged necessary at any time, by the nursing staff unilaterally should the doctor not be immediately available for consultation. The general aim should be to ensure clinical improvement such that progressive reductions in the level of supportive observation occur as rapidly as possible. If there is any doubt concerning the appropriate level of supportive observation, consultation with more senior staff should take place.

8.15 A number of general points need to be borne in mind when carrying out the more intensive levels of supportive observation. If the suicidal patient feels too crowded by the hospital staff, there is a danger of suicidal behaviour being provoked. Alternatively, if the patient obtains secondary gain from close attention, suicidal behaviour may be inadvertently reinforced. If supportive observation is equated with surveillance as part of a rigid regime, the patient's rights and needs will be ignored and stigmatisation is inevitable. **Supportive observation should be seen as a therapeutic plan rather than custodial care.** The focus should be on gaining good rapport with the patient, promoting coping skills and being aware of individual personal needs. When carried out appropriately, intensive supportive observation allows sensitive monitoring of the patient's behaviour and mental state and a rapid response to any change, whilst at the same time fostering positive therapeutic relationships. Both the patient and staff should feel, and actually be, safer. If the staff complement is limited, either in terms of number or seniority, all efforts should be made to ensure that other patients on the ward continue to receive a fair share of the overall ward resources. The whole approach relies on establishing an alliance which is welcomed by the patient. The less intensive levels of supportive observation are especially dependent on co-operation between patient and staff in order to achieve their full effectiveness. Whatever level is implemented, **it must be remembered that suicide risk is only one aspect of any clinical problem. Other potential risks, such as aggressive behaviour, should also be evaluated and managed, in order to ensure safety of other patients as well as staff.**

8.16 Every effort should be made to ensure that the process of observation does not compromise the patient's sense of privacy, autonomy and dignity. The paramount aim should be to develop a close, supportive relationship.

8.17 The following features should be observed and any changes that occur noted. A full systematic assessment of the individual's mental state should be carried out regularly. It is easy, otherwise, to miss morbid ideas.

a. appearance.

b. general behaviour, level of co-operation, acceptance of help.

c. morbid ideas, especially depressive self-blame, hopelessness about the future, suicidal intent.

d. mood and attitude.

e. orientation, awareness, memory function.

f. insight into present situation.

8.18 Staff should distinguish and record those observations which are subjective and those which are objective. A statement such as 'patient is suicidal' is less useful than one which indicates whether it is based entirely on what the patient says as opposed to conclusions reached by a staff member from observations made of the patient.

8.19 The role of each staff member should be outlined in the light of their skills and experience.

1. Constant Supportive Observation (Level One)

8.20 *A designated nurse keeps the patient under constant visual observation. This may be relaxed for short periods, for example, toilet purposes. A specific decision should be made, after discussion between medical and nursing staff, as to whether the patient should be ambulant or be nursed in bed for a while and use a bedside commode as opposed to the normal ward toilet facilities. If the latter, then the patient should not be able to lock or otherwise barricade him or herself in and prevent staff access, as necessary, and the nurse should remain nearby. This level of observation can be carried out in the observation area of an open psychiatric admission unit, but care should be taken to ensure that levels of nursing staff are adequate, particularly at night, so that the level of care can be maintained throughout the 24-hour period. Regular review and control of dangerous items in the vicinity of the patient is required. If the patient leaves the ward for any reason, for example, to attend occupational therapy, this should be in the company of the designated nurse who should remain with the patient at all times whilst he or she is outside the ward. The patient should not be granted leave.*

8.21 The role of designated nurse may need to rotate regularly between staff members so that any emotional stress is not placed too heavily on one person. Due regard, however, should be given to the advantages of continuity of care and the patient being able to form trusting relationships. There should be no ambiguity with regard to who is the designated nurse at any time and all staff involved should share an agreed thera-

peutic approach. At all times, the risk to staff as a result of aggressive behaviour should be taken into consideration. This is particularly important in the case of impulsive, irritable patients and those whose behaviour is related to psychotic illness with delusional ideas, as their behaviour is not easy to predict.

8.22 If the patient is impulsive and assessed as being at serious suicide risk, the designated nurse, or nurses if this is thought necessary to ensure safety of staff, should remain physically close to the patient who may be confined to bed for short periods if the situation cannot otherwise be contained. This level may be termed *constant nearby supportive observation, or level 1 A.* Although very infrequently necessary, it does represent an option which should be used if the clinical situation demands it.

8.23 The types of patient for whom *constant supportive observation* is appropriate might include those expressing active suicidal intent, especially if no close relationship has been established with the patient, those in unpredictable psychotic states or where there has been a recent episode of deliberate self-harm with apparent serious suicidal intent. *This is not a prescriptive list. The level of supportive observation chosen depends upon careful assessment of the differential weightings of risk factors in each individual. Special care should be taken if the patient is impulsive or aggressive.*

2. Fifteen Minute Supportive Observation (Level Two)

8.24 *A designated nurse maintains intermittent visual contact with the patient at intervals, which, on average, are not more than fifteen-minutes. It is useful to randomise the exact timing of observation by varying it from ten minutes to twenty minutes. There should be regular assessment of the mental state of the patient, who should undertake to keep the nurse informed about his or her whereabouts. The patient should not leave the ward by him or herself, but is allowed to visit the toilet unaccompanied or remain in the company of relatives for short periods. Relatives should be warned that they are expected to tell staff when they leave the patient's company. The patient should sleep at night in the ward observation area. The patient is accompanied by a nurse when leaving the ward for any purpose, and other staff, for example, occupational therapists and social workers, should be aware of the level of observation required. It may be necessary for the designated nurse to remain with such a patient when visiting any other hospital department if the desired level of observation is to be maintained. No leave should be granted to the patient. This level of care depends a great deal on the patient's co-operation; the patient should feel able to welcome the intensive support from staff rather than resent it. It follows also that a good lasting relationship and alliance between staff and patient renders the whole process more effective.*

8.25 The types of patient for whom this level of care is appropriate might include those where a close relationship has been established between the patient and staff, and where the patient is judged not to be actively suicidal but is considered to be at significantly greater suicide risk compared with the average psychiatric inpatient. For example, it might be used where there has been a recent incident of deliberate self-harm with some degree of suicidal intent, or where there are current major stressors, or depressive features. It might also be appropriate for such a patient in a medical ward awaiting transfer to a psychiatric ward, if agreed by all staff concerned. *This is not a prescriptive list; the precise level of supportive obser-*

vation depends on the careful assessment of differential weightings of risk factors in each individual.

3. Known Place Supportive Observation (Level Three)

8.26 *A designated nurse knows the whereabouts of the patient. Occupational therapy and other departments should be informed when the patient leaves the ward in order to attend there. The patient may be allowed to leave the ward for short periods (10-15 minutes) unaccompanied but should keep the nursing staff informed about details of such arrangements. Any failure to keep to an agreed plan should indicate an immediate review of the level of supportive observation. This level is appropriate for the dormitory area of an admission ward. Leave is granted only with caution. It depends heavily upon a good relationship and alliance with the patient for its full effectiveness.*

8.27 This level of supportive observation might be used for high risk category patients who are not actively suicidal and are judged to be free from immediate significant suicidal risk. It is commonly utilised during recovery from a suicidal crisis. Staff should bear in mind the possibility of false improvement when deciding upon this lower level of supportive observation. *This is not a prescriptive list; the precise level of supportive observation depends on the careful assessment of differential weightings of risk factors in each individual.*

Continuing Care

8.28 **Throughout the period of care, clear documentation and communication are essential to provide a universally understood and well co-ordinated approach.** Discussion with, and explanation to, the patient are also vital at all times. It should be made clear to the patient that he or she will be involved, as far as possible, in decisions on clinical management and can approach staff at any time, particularly if he or she is feeling distressed. Willingness to discuss suicidal ideas should be encouraged. Several types of problem need to be addressed with the patient, including individual psychological processes as well as behavioural, medical, interpersonal, family and social issues. All members of staff should be aware of the phenomenon of 'misleading improvement' which can occur merely by admitting suicidal patients to hospital and thus removing them from stressful situations. Rapid relapse can occur on return to the community, unless adverse factors have been resolved or appropriately addressed by ensuring that the patient really can cope with them. Staff should also be aware of the risk of malignant alienation in patients whose behaviour is challenging or difficult. Where possible, relatives and 'key others' should be involved in the process of care.

8.29 Setting limits may well be necessary but such clinical decisions are amongst the most difficult and staff cohesion is essential to get them right. Personality-disordered persons who present challenging behaviour in the absence of florid mental illness are perhaps the most difficult of all to assess and manage. On the one hand, on-going management has to set limits as to acceptable behaviour, and it is necessary to come to a decision about what should be expected from voluntary control on the part of the patient. Yet on the other hand, in crisis, especially when alcohol intoxication complicates the picture, such persons can kill themselves and it can be very difficult indeed to know how rigorously to intervene. Clinical decisions in such circum-

stances are more likely to be right if rigid rules are avoided. It should be recognised that some people with difficult personalities and challenging behaviour may at times of crisis be at significant risk, their judgement impaired, and so be in need of vigorous short-term intervention if suicide is to be avoided.

Visitors and Leave

8.30 The frequency and length of visits from relatives and key other persons should be discussed with the patient and assessed in terms of their appropriateness. The aim should be to maximise the patient's care and support and to promote the resolution of interpersonal issues without exposing the patient to undue stress. It can help if such visitors are given a brief explanation of the patient's current state – as a general rule with the patient's permission and preferably while the patient is present – but with due consideration to issues of confidentiality and the patient's self-respect. In certain circumstances, gifts from visitors may need to be vetted by staff for possible danger. It is often appropriate for other key people to be perceived by staff as playing a significant part in enacting an overall treatment programme.

8.31 One recent study[1] found that more than one-third of 'inpatient' suicides occurred while the patient was on leave from the ward. When significant suicide risk has been present in the recent past, leave should only be granted after full discussion with the patient, ward staff, and the patient's family or carers. Suicide risk should be judged to be manageable. Special care should be taken if the patient is returning to stressors that he or she has been protected from in the hospital environment. The recovery phase of a depres-

---

[1] Morgan & Priest, 1991.

sive illness should also be regarded with caution, as suicide can result if the level of activity and drive improves before negative thoughts have disappeared. When there is danger of overdose, medication needs to be prescribed safely and the patient should be given a contact telephone number and a person to call if he or she becomes acutely suicidal whilst on leave. It should be made clear to the patient that he or she can contact the hospital or return to the ward at any time. The patient's family or carers should be given time to ventilate any worries. It can be useful to advise them how to watch out for signs of deterioration in their relative's mental state and to ensure that they, too, have a contact telephone number of persons to call if they have any cause for concern. On return from leave, the patient's management plan can be reviewed after discussing the leave period with the individual and his or her family or carers. In the case of patients who have been detained under a Section of the 1983 Mental Health Act great care should be taken to ensure that leave arrangements comply with the Act's requirements. For example, Section 17 directs that the consultant who has the role of Responsible Medical Officer must give specific permission for any leave, and restriction orders need necessarily to involve close liaison with the Home Office. Section 17 documentation should include forms which are readily available in the case-notes, enabling specific details of the agreed leave to be indicated unequivocally by the relevant Responsible Medical Officer.

Untoward Events

8.32 If a patient harms him or herself or is suspected of having taken an overdose, a doctor should be called immediately and appropriate medical action should be taken. If any doubt exists as to whether an overdose has been taken, caution should prevail and transfer to a general hospital should be arranged. Any such transfer should ideally occur with a nurse escort and a clear communication to the general hospital as to the psychological and medical problems. If admission to a general hospital is required, advisory guidelines for appropriate psychiatric management in that setting need to be provided by the psychiatric or mental health team involved, and regular review of the patient's mental state arranged.

8.33 As soon as possible after the act of deliberate self-harm, the degree of suicidal intent should be assessed, together with the motivation behind the act and any possible precipitants. In the light of this, the level of supportive observation and the management plan should be reviewed. Ward policy should be reviewed in the light of the events to see if there are any general lessons to be learned.

8.34 If a patient at risk of suicide is thought to have gone absent without leave from the ward, the nurse in charge plus the relevant medical staff should be informed immediately. A thorough search of the ward, the hospital and its grounds should take place at once according to established search procedures. Family and carers should be informed of events and asked to contact the hospital if they see or hear of the patient. The police should be issued with an accurate description of the patient and informed of the possible risks.

8.35 On return to the ward, the patient should be questioned as to his or her motivation for going absent in this way. It is wise to remember that a patient may go absent without leave when feeling suicidal, yet on return may already feel better. Assessment should take into account the variability in degree of suicidal ideation which is so common in suicidal individuals. In the light of this, the level of observation and management plan should be reviewed, and, as for an episode of DSH, ward policy should also be reviewed.

Ward Transfer

8.36 The period following any change of inpatient setting is a vulnerable time for suicidal patients, as the trust and rapport that have developed with one set of staff is lost and the patient is required to engage with a new group of people. This can be a significant loss for the patient and may be perceived as rejection and a blow to self-esteem. This stress can be minimised by giving as much warning as possible of the transfer, so that the patient can begin to come to terms with the change. It is extremely useful if staff from the new ward can visit the patient to gain some trust prior to the transfer. Visiting the new ward before the move can also make the transfer less threatening. The point of view of the patient should be considered in detail, and taken into account as far as it is possible to do so.

8.37 Clear communication of all aspects of the patient's care between members of each discipline is essential. The exact time of transfer should be arranged and agreed to be when both wards are least busy. The patient should be escorted between wards and a staff member on the new ward should be available to welcome the patient and introduce him or her to the ward. The level of supportive observation that was necessary up to the point of transfer needs to be made clear to the staff of the receiving ward and the level required in the new ward decided without delay. It may need to be intensified during the initial phase following transfer. If the patient moves to a dif-

ferent hospital, care should be taken to ensure that there is no ambiguity in terminology of care procedures, especially with regard to the level of supportive observation.

Discharge

8.38 **The first few weeks after discharge represent a period of greatly increased risk of suicide.** The patient may have left a relatively protective and supportive environment to face unresolved stressors. The patient may also perceive that his or her hospital stay has failed to help and that discharge represents abandonment and rejection. This is a particular worry if any depressive features are still apparent. These issues should be discussed with the patient and his or her family and carers prior to discharge.

8.39 The discharge date should, ideally, be agreed at least several days in advance so that the patient can come to terms with the idea. The co-ordinated team approach sets the scene for the planning of care programmes[2] in anticipation of discharge from hospital. Medication should be prescribed in safe amounts. A follow-up appointment needs to be made as soon as possible after discharge, preferably with someone the patient knows well and trusts. The patient and his or her family and carers should be aware of how to obtain help if it is required prior to the follow-up appointment.

8.40 The development of community care should not be at the expense of providing adequate inpatient facilities, which can be seen as the equivalent of intensive care in general medicine, for those who really need supportive observation and treatment greater than that which can be provided in the community. Excessive reduction of bed numbers

---

[2] Department of Health, 1990.

can, in certain circumstances, mean that patients who need admission are denied it, or that they are discharged prematurely to make way for other admissions. The hazard of this is increased by the fact that clinical improvement often occurs prior to suicide in certain psychiatric patients. For example, as Table 9 below illustrates, in one study[1] almost half of a series of psychiatric patients who committed suicide, either whilst in hospital or soon afterwards, had shown clinical improvement: it was a misleading clinical finding especially as the underlying problems had remained unresolved in more than 80% of these patients.

Table Nine

27 Suicides amongst psychiatric inpatients in Avon

(during admission or within 2 months of discharge)

Suicide risk discussed at some time:	21
Precautions taken to prevent suicide:	11
Allowed on leave or move to outpatient or day patient status:	11
Able to absent themselves without leave:	13
Suicide on ward itself:	3
Significant clinical improvement:	14
(Problem unresolved	12)
Alienation	15

8.41 Although 74% had been recognised as presenting a suicide risk, only in 40% were specific precautions taken. 85% of the suicides occurred outside the ward setting, often when the patient had been allowed out on leave. The paradoxical finding that the period immediately following discharge from hospital is a time of increased suicide risk may itself in some degree reflect these various problems.

8.42 The preceding paragraphs have illustrated some of the problems encountered in the management of suicide risk in hospital. These are presented in summary form in Check-List 14 (page 117).

[1] Morgan & Priest, 1991.

Chapter Nine

A Problem-Solving Approach

9.1　To be fully effective in helping to resolve a suicidal crisis, it is necessary to have a thorough knowledge of all the facts through a full clinical history, and this should ideally involve interviews with key others as well as with the person concerned, a full psychological and behavioural assessment, followed by a diagnostic formulation and identification of aetiological factors leading finally to the establishment of a treatment plan. There are many possible choices of clinical management in attempting to resolve suicide risk and these depend upon the diagnostic formulation: approaches may vary from those which emphasise physical treatment (such as medication) through to different forms of psychological and social therapy. Ideally, a comprehensive approach involves a judicious use of several strategies concurrently.

9.2　Quite often a therapist feels at a loss as to how to structure the way in which he or she addresses the ongoing problems of suicidal ideation and behaviour. It is here that a problem-solving approach, derived from cognitive behavioural theory, can help in establishing a coherent aim and momentum in the therapeutic effort. Key cognitive and behavioural aspects of suicide risk (for example, specific cognitive distortions and the central role of hopelessness and helplessness as precursors of suicidal despair) have been identified,[1] thereby offering a therapeutic framework to structure what needs to be done.

9.3　**Such a problem-solving approach can be very useful, particularly in facilitating other strategies, and is** **not in any way exclusive.** Problem-solving buffers the debilitating effect of negative events. It is based on the assumption that when problem-solving fails – and it can do so for a large variety of reasons – then hopelessness or helplessness supervene leading to suicidal behaviour.

9.4　Problem-solving aims to help identify life situations which provoke suicidal behaviour and to minimise the negative impact of hopelessness on current and future coping attempts. It seeks to increase the effectiveness of the individual's ability to solve problems and challenge cognitive distortions. It targets certain specific cognitive distortions which feature commonly in the suicidal state of mind. The following two examples demonstrate this approach.

Hopelessness

The focus of the work is to:
- encourage the patient to view hopelessness as a symptom
- guide the patient to see that negative expectations may not be an accurate reflection of reality
- list the goals or problems which underpin hopelessness
- guide the patient to see that other interpretations and actions are possible

View of Suicide as 'Desirable'

The focus of the work is to:
- help the patient to identify reasons for dying or living
- encourage a careful appraisal of those reasons
- list the perceived disadvantages and advantages of suicide

[1] Beck et al, 1979.

- strengthen reasons for living and correct any cognitive distortions about the advantages of dying

9.5 Problem-solving involves:

   a. the recognition and admission that a problem exists;

   b. being able to communicate this to appropriate others;

   c. the generation of alternative solutions other than suicide;

   d. the implementation of a solution;

   e. assessing the outcome.

9.6 The Defeat Depression Campaign, organised by the Royal College of Psychiatrists in association with the Royal College of General Practitioners, supports an eclectic approach to the management of people with depression. The campaign has launched an audio tape programme, 'Coping with Depression', which includes cognitive therapy techniques appropriate for use in combating the effects of depression.

9.7 It is impossible to do justice to the cognitive behavioural approach to suicide risk within the limits of this, essentially brief, text. It is a most valuable approach, not least because it provides a framework which can facilitate the establishment of a therapeutic alliance between a patient and a therapist. It should not be used, however, to the exclusion of other approaches. For example, the profoundly depressed individual with nihilistic or other delusions, or a person who suffers from schizophrenic-type delusional ideas might experience worsening of despair if challenged cognitively at a time when he or she finds it impossible to respond and when physical treatments are probably more appropriate. Close multidisciplinary collaboration is essential to make sure that all aspects relevant to any problem of suicide risk are addressed effectively and in a co-ordinated, integrated way. The problem-solving approach can also be applied in group work.[2]

---

[2] Fraser, 1986.

Chapter Ten

Suicide Risk Questionnaires

10.1 Suicide, as previously discussed, is an uncommon event which is difficult to predict. In an attempt to improve capabilities in this area, a number of suicide risk scales have been devised which aim to discriminate between individuals who will at some period in the future commit suicide (or engage in suicidal behaviour) and those who will not. These scales vary in their clinical usefulness but at times can be helpful tools in gauging the degree of suicide risk or monitoring any change in it.

10.2 Use of scales, however, should never replace a thorough psychiatric assessment and mental state examination. At most, they should be used as an adjunct to the clinical evaluation of risk. It should be remembered that such scales have been designed by estimating the rate of suicide in a population over an extended period of time; they are far less effective in measuring an individual person's short-term risk in an acute clinical setting. Regular use, however, may be helpful in monitoring progress.

10.3 Most suicide risk scales take the form of a questionnaire against which the rater scores a number of variables. The areas covered generally include demographic data, previous history, social adjustment, psychopathology and psychiatric diagnosis.

10.4 In a perfect world, a scale would discriminate correctly between all suicides and non-suicides. In reality, this is virtually impossible to achieve. If a cut-off score is chosen so that all suicides are predicted correctly, this group will inevitably contain a high number of non-suicides. Alternatively if a cut-off score is chosen to minimise the number of wrongly allocated non-suicides, there is a risk that fewer suicides will be correctly predicted.

10.5 The sensitivity and specificity of a risk scale are measures of how well a scale can discriminate between the two groups and these values are defined:

- **sensitivity** = $\dfrac{\text{true positives}}{\text{true positives} + \text{false positives}}$;

- **specificity** = $\dfrac{\text{true negatives}}{\text{true negatives} + \text{false negatives}}$.

10.6 Ideally, both sensitivity and specificity would be 1, but in the case of suicide risk scales high sensitivity is associated with low specificity and vice versa.

10.7 There are a number of other factors to be considered when deciding how valuable a particular risk scale is. These are:

The population studied in deriving the scale (eg cases of DSH, psychiatric inpatients).

The method of data collection and analysis used in deriving the scale (eg the size of the population studied, whether studied prospectively or retrospectively, statistical methods used etc).

The event to be predicted (eg suicide, DSH).

The time taken to administer the scale.

Inter-rater and re-test reliability.

A scale should, ideally, be used only on the same population as that used in its derivation.

10.8 The following are examples of scales which have been found to be of value in assessing suicide risk. Full references are given in the bibliography for those specifically interested in this subject.

Table Ten

Suicide Risk Questionnaires

Hopelessness scale (Beck et al, 1985).

Suicidal intent scale (Beck et al, 1974).

6 & 18 Item risk scale DSH (Pallis et al 1982).

Suicide prediction schedule for neuro-psychiatric hospital patients (Faberow & MacKinnon, 1974).

Scale for estimation of suicidal risk – psychiatric inpatient (Motto & Heilbron, 1976).

PATHOS Screening questionnaire (for adolescents after DSH) (Kingsbury, 1993).

PART C

A

SELECTION OF

VULNERABLE GROUPS

Chapter Eleven

Adolescents

11.1 The loss of life as a result of suicide is always a tragedy for those concerned. The suicide of a young person, however, seems all the more distressing, not only because of the waste of a life hardly begun, but also because of the burden of responsibility carried by the adults closely connected with that individual.

11.2 Adolescent suicide has been much in the news in the recent past. Suicide among young people is a phenomenon both puzzling and worrying. The rates of male suicide in all age groups and in most countries have shown a striking increase since the 1970s but this is most marked in the 15-24 year age group. By the mid-1980s in Britain and in almost all European countries, as well as in the United States, suicide among young people was markedly greater than in the previous decade.[1] In many parts of the world it had become the second most frequent cause of death, after accident, among the 15-24 year age group.

11.3 Figures for England and Wales, comparing the period 1970-74 with 1980-84, show a 43% increase in male suicide among young people, and a 25% decrease for females in the same age group. The most recent figures compare the period 1976-81 with 1986-91 and are shown in Table 11 below:

Table Eleven

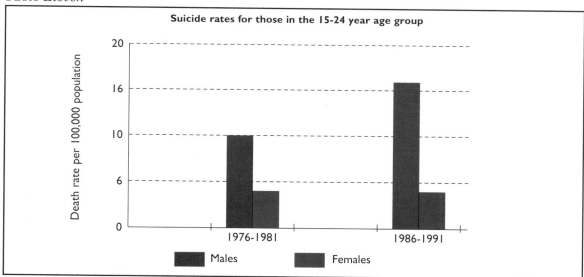

These show male suicides in the 15-24 year age group have increased from just under 10 per 100,000 population to approximately 16 per 100,000, a 60% increase. The figures for young women show no change at all, the rate remaining at just under 5 per 100,000. Thus, not only has there been a continuing increase in young male suicide rates, but, in addition, young men are three times more likely to commit suicide than are young women. However, in cases of deliberate self-harm (DSH), young women outnumber men quite substantially (see paras 11.8 to 11.17).

[1] McClure, 1986.

Gender Differences

11.4 A number of possible explanations have been advanced for the gender difference in completed suicide rates amongst young people. It has been known for some time that aggressive and anti-social behaviour, alcohol abuse and depression in young people are risk factors for eventual suicide. There are substantial differences between boys and girls in their susceptibility to these risk factors with girls being more likely to suffer depression and boys at greater risk of alcohol and substance abuse, especially as rates of alcoholism and substance abuse have increased amongst young people over the last two decades in close parallel with the increase in suicide rates in that age group.

11.5 Other reasons which may explain the gender difference include the predilection for more lethal methods of self-harm shown by boys; this parallels the higher rate of risk-taking behaviour amongst boys, leading them to a greater familiarity with lethal techniques. This risk-taking behaviour has been linked with increasing adolescent male concerns about keeping up with contemporary 'tough guy' masculine stereotypes[2]. Another factor may be the differing cultural sanctions on the expression of emotion by males and females.[3] There is an expectation that boys will display less emotion than girls such that girls appear to have more freedom to express and communicate feelings. This may be linked to their being less likely to use lethal means to express distress in a self-injurious manner.

Risk Factors

11.6 In considering the increase in suicide rates amongst young people, there is a number of specific risk factors which need to be considered:

a. **Economic and Social Pressures.** Much has been made of economic factors; in particular, growing unemployment amongst young men is often cited as one possible cause for increased suicide rates. However, the upward trend is occurring in almost all Western countries, whatever their economic situation, and furthermore, the trend is long-standing, extending now to a period of almost 20 years.[4] It is therefore generally agreed[5] that, while unemployment, and especially the poverty associated with it, may be one contributory factor in the aetiology of youth suicide, it is only one among many. The enormous structural changes taking place in the family, and fragmented career paths, are further possible factors.

b. **Alcohol and Substance Abuse.** It is clear that alcohol and substance abuse are significant risk factors. They affect all areas of functioning, and may act as an immediate precipitant to suicide due to decreased inhibitions.[6] Approximately one in three adolescents who commit suicide is intoxicated at the time of death, and a further number are under the influence of drugs.[7] It has been found that the percentage change in alcohol consumption has the single highest correlation with changes in suicide rates.[8] The implications for prevention and intervention are clear: **focusing on drug and alcohol abuse would have a greater impact on adolescent suicide rates than any other primary prevention programme.**

[2] Hill & Lynch, 1993.
[3] Berman & Jobes, 1991.
[4] Bingham et al, 1994.
[5] Garland & Zigler, 1992.
[6] Shaffer, 1988.
[7] Brent et al, 1988.
[8] Diekstra, 1989.

c. **Custody.**

There have been a number of high-profile cases in the UK in recent years in which young men, often on remand, have killed themselves while in young offender institutions. This has led to much public anxiety. Chapter 13 deals specifically with prisoners but it is worth noting here, in relation to adolescents and young people, that within the prison population as a whole, young prisoners represent the largest group of at-risk individuals, especially those under 21. They make up a third of the remand population – a group known to be at increased risk of suicide – and, although their stay in custody may be relatively short, the size of the young offender remand population has increased far more over the last 20 years than the adult remand population. Young prisoner suicides are more likely to cluster in particular establishments and they are more likely to occur at earlier stages in the custodial process.

d. **Bullying.**

A small number of children and adolescents each year make a serious suicide attempt as a direct consequence of being bullied at school, and there are occasional reports of similar peer abuse driving male recruits in the armed forces to suicide. A number of schools have relatively recently introduced anti-bullying policies but there has been little study of which groups are especially vulnerable.

Typically, children who are victims of bullying do not disclose it to parents and teachers, or are met with dismissive responses if they do. There is a suspicion that teenagers with special educational needs are vulnerable and some indications that children in special needs units housed in mainstream schools may be particularly vulnerable. Doctors and others who are involved with children with special educational needs should ask them directly about experiences of bullying and, if appropriate, advise their parents to take the matter up firmly with the school.

e. **Rural Isolation.**

While there is evidence[9] that rural life can in some way contribute to high levels of suicide, particularly amongst those who are socially isolated, there is, as yet, insufficient evidence to indicate whether this general finding is applicable to the adolescent and young adult age group. This is an area requiring further research.

f. **Physical and Sexual Abuse.**

Young people who suffer, or have suffered in the past, from physical or sexual abuse are often at increased risk of suicide or deliberate self-harm. Like running away from home, an act of DSH can be a dangerous but effective way of escaping from an abusing situation, as removal to hospital following the DSH can ensure that the abused child has a safe distance placed between him or herself and the abuser.

11.7 Methods of suicide amongst adolescents and young people have reflected the changes of method for suicides as a whole (see para 3.4). There is no evidence that there are differences in choice of method in the 15-24 age group compared with suicides of all ages. As with all suicides, psychological autopsy

---

[9] Gallagher & Sheehy, 1994.

shows a high rate of psychiatric disorder amongst young people who commit suicide.

Deliberate Self-harm

11.8 It is necessary to consider deliberate self-harm when discussing suicide, even though the former is, by definition, not lethal. As is the case with adults, there is some potential confusion over terminology. In relation to young people the term deliberate self-harm (DSH) is used throughout and includes parasuicide, deliberate self-harm, deliberate self-poisoning and attempted suicide.

11.9 In DSH, the gender difference between males and females is precisely the reverse of that for completed suicides, with young women being three to four times more likely to become involved in these types of action than their male counterparts.[10] The rate of adolescent overdose is increasing, especially among older adolescent girls.[11] The vast majority of DSH behaviour in young people in this country involves intentional overdoses. Most of these are not fully suicidal but some young people will have been suicidal at the time they took the overdose and their acts are true attempts at suicide. Wrist and forearm cutting may co-exist with overdosing but is essentially a different phenomenon and very unlikely to prove lethal. It is not considered further here.

11.10 Intentional overdosing may prove lethal because the dose or agent is misjudged so that the final death is recorded as suicide, because the agent was consciously self-administered, yet suicidal motivation may vary enormously among overdosers and for some may

have been minimal. **Follow-up studies of teenagers who take overdoses show that up to 11% will die by their own hand over the next few years.** Some of these will die by mistake and some will fully intend to do so. Adolescents who harm themselves fall into two groups, one psychologically indistinguishable from completed suicides; the other group is made up of people who show more impulsive behaviour and conform to the public notion of the adolescent overdoser as a person who is feeling desperate and wants others to notice and intervene.[12]

11.11 Suicidal behaviour and acts of DSH must be considered in relation to the family context and the overall context of adolescent development. It is in the important transitional process from childhood to maturity that a sociological perspective becomes important. It highlights two important and linked concepts, namely, *socialisation* and *role*. When viewed within a developmental perspective, adolescent suicidal behaviour may be seen as arising from failures in socialisation, and failures in role performance and role transition. Features of adolescent development such as the growth of capacity for mutual dependency, greater involvement with peer groups, and sensitivity to the evaluations of others, all provoke role transitions. Paradoxically, at a time when adolescents are striving to develop personal autonomy, the change and uncertainty this produces is likely to increase their dependence on others for reassurance and support. In addition, major environmental changes such as progression through school, moving into employment, and leaving home, all demand involvement in new sets of relationships. Some of the problems which provoke suicidal behaviour

---

[10] Kerfoot, 1988.

[11] Hawton & Fagg, 1992.

[12] Hawton et al, 1982.

and DSH in adolescents reflect their feelings of lack of success or actual failures in these critical areas.

11.12 The backgrounds of adolescents who deliberately harm themselves are characterised by a high degree of family problems. Compared with other teenagers,[13] this group has more rows with both parents and, particularly, difficulties with their fathers. Many of these young people have had frequent contact with helping agencies before they commit an act of DSH, especially with social workers or general practitioners, and significant numbers (in the region of one-third) have taken a previous overdose. For many, there is a specific event superimposed upon more chronic difficulties that is felt to be the last straw which precipitates the taking of the overdose or other act of DSH. In the majority this is a row either with parents or with a boy- or girl-friend. Although in the minority there is no clear 'last straw', it is in this minority that a psychiatric disorder is most often found. It is important not to be distracted by the contribution of the 'last straw' when assessing suicide risk. Despite the general pervasiveness among this group of young people of feelings of distress, loneliness and anger, it seems to be the case that many overdoses are impulsive. Most do not plan at all, taking handfuls of whatever is available and only a small minority plan their overdose more than three hours in advance.

11.13 Strikingly, the great majority appear to have little sustained suicidal intent. Very few overdoses take place with no-one else in the house, and many occur with a family member in a nearby room. Frequently, not all the medication that is available is taken, and

many young people tell someone what has happened shortly after the incident. Few leave suicide notes and few make any attempt to conceal their self-destructive behaviour.

11.14 Amongst females of all ages, Asian women are over-represented in self-poisoning.[14] This is also true of the 15-19 year age group. It has been shown that the most important factors in the DSH behaviour of Asian adolescents are cultural conflicts rather than factors associated with a disruptive family background. Little difference, however, is found between Asians and other people in the type of poisoning or the degree of pre-planning involved. Asians who commit acts of DSH have been shown[15] to be more socially isolated and, despite having low suicidal intent, they have higher rates of depression, hopelessness, longer premeditation time and higher rates of previous overdose. This suggests that the clinical assessment of Asian adolescents who overdose should rely less heavily on the evaluation of suicidal intent than is appropriate for other groups.

11.15 There is an eventual mortality rate associated with DSH of up to 11% of young people who overdose going on to kill themselves later.[16] There is also a significant repetition rate of 10% within 12 months of the original episode and a continuing risk of further episodes.[17] These rates must be borne in mind when assessing and preparing a management plan for an adolescent who has committed an act of DSH. Although it is commonly said that adolescent overdosing is a communication – a cry for help – or manipulative, there is a danger that such terms trivialise the issue by focusing on the last straw precipitant rather than the back-

---

[13] Kingsbury, 1993.
[14] Merrill & Owens, 1986.
[15] Kingsbury, 1994.
[16] Kotila & Longquist, 1989.
[17] Kerfoot and McHugh, 1992.

ground factors. Significant rates of psychiatric disorder have been found to be present at the time of an overdose. The rates of depression are high – higher even than amongst completed suicides in some studies – but rates of substance abuse and anti-social behaviour are relatively lower. Recent reports, however, suggest that the rates for substance abuse in particular are rising (Buckstein et al, 1993). Rates of previous or current intra-familial abuse are considerably higher than in the general population.

11.16 In considering DSH, it is helpful to have certain premises in mind:

- DSH arises out of relationship problems which are in crisis.

- DSH is a communication that the crisis feels to be beyond the control of the subject.

- DSH is a metaphor for problems of hostility, loss and responsibility.

- DSH is an attempted solution.

11.17 Reducing the level of overdoses, it is reasonable to assume, would lower the suicide rate. Even though the majority of those who overdose have relatively little suicidal intent, there is a proportion that proves lethal. One approach would be to take measures to reduce the toxicity of some of the commonest agents. Paracetamol is, for example, potentially lethal because of its effect on the liver. It could be dispensed in ways which would make it harder to obtain or harder to accumulate a lethal dose, such as by blister packaging. Paracetamol could be combined in its preparation with an emetic so that an excessive dose would be vomited up before entering the blood stream or it could be combined with methionine to alleviate liver damage.

Risk Assessment after DSH

11.18 A thorough psychiatric assessment is very important as is hospital admission, if at all possible; this allows for fuller assessment than in an Accident and Emergency Department, enables risk in the young person's living situation (eg abuse) to be assessed and allows for the patient who conceals the extent of the overdose and counteracts the common tendency of anxious, guilty parents to play down the significance of the act. It is also important that staff dealing with adolescents from whatever background have appropriate training. Central to the assessment of DSH are the need to understand why and when the DSH took place and an examination of the mental state of the young person, including an assessment of suicide risk and the likelihood of repetition. It is important that Accident and Emergency Department staff are trained to recognise that a conscious teenager, frightened by the consequences of his or her behaviour, may lie as to what he or she has done and minimise the quantity of tablets taken. The final precipitant for the act is often trivial and thus can mislead anyone who does not probe the background. A girl who is being sexually abused within her family, for example, may take an overdose after a minor row with her mother. Manipulative behaviour as a motive for DSH is unusual among adolescents, though it is often attributed by untrained staff. Nor are terms such as "attention-seeking" or "a cry for help" helpful in that they do not fully or accurately reflect motivation.

11.19 The assessment of an adolescent who has taken an overdose should involve direct questioning about physical and sexual abuse. It must also include an assessment as to whether the family environment to which the adolescent will return can provide adequate protection. For such reasons, facilities for interviewing in private must be available – drawing curtains around the bed on a public ward is insufficient. Because of the existence of abuse in a small but appreciable minority of cases, any assessment needs to check whether the adolescent is registered on the local child protection register. This may not always be administratively straightforward, but it is important that it is done. Examination of the individual's mental state may reveal a disorder, such as depression, which can be treated in its own right by cognitive therapy or anti-depressants (though only those that are relatively safe in overdose in case the DSH is repeated).

11.20 To ensure that the assessment is full and thorough, it may be helpful to draw up and use a check-list of good practice, designed to address both the general and specific aspects of assessment. The check-list should serve two main purposes. First, it should meet the needs of assessment by providing sufficient and appropriate information to allow clinicians to answer the questions they have set themselves, and to make judgements about how to proceed. Second, it should act as a data-gathering instrument for the purposes of clinical audit (see Chapter 17), service evaluation, and research. It may be helpful for such lists to be developed locally so that they can be tailored to meet local needs in ways which are sensitive to the local situation: frequent usage can identify any difficulties in its application and allow for fine tuning. Table 12 below (and reproduced in Chapter 20 as Check-List 7 (pages 109 and 110)) summarises the key areas for assessment with suicidal adolescents and their families, and provides a basis for local practice.

Table Twelve

Assessment of DSH (Children and Adolescents)

Key Areas in Assessment	
Circumstances of the episode of DSH	• method used • source of agent • availability • likelihood of discovery • suicidal communications • motives • precipitants • previous acts of DSH
Social life and activities	• network of relationships • out of school activities • casual or close friendships • dating • leisure activities • degree of freedom from parental authority and intrusion
School (where applicable)	• time in school • changes of school • attendance record • work record • behaviour in relation to staff and peers • bullying
Problems and coping strategies	• current problem behaviours, eg delinquency • anxieties, eg school, running away, physical, sexual or emotional abuse • alcohol or drug abuse

General health	• previous significant medical history
	• present health status
	• psychiatric status including specifically:
	  – variation in sleep patterns
	  – appetite
	  – mood
	• health contacts, eg GP, clinic or hospital appointments
	• current treatments

Family structure and relationships	• marital status of parents • composition of family • rating of relationships within the family • emotional climate in the home • expressed emotions (EE) • frequency and pattern of arguments • past or present abuse
Family circumstances	• level of income • housing • environmental problems • family pathology, eg crime, mental illness • family history of suicide • physical or mental disability • contacts with social agencies
Other higher risk items	• others not present or nearby at the time • intervention unlikely • precautions taken against discovery • suicide note • problems for longer than a month • episode planned for more than three hours • feeling hopeless about the future • feeling sad most of the time prior to the act of DSH • contributing social or family adversity • use of alcohol or drugs

11.21 Often, there is no clear or obvious link between the act of DSH and a second overdose or suicide attempt by other means, and prediction is fraught with difficulties. However, there is some evidence that the longer both behavioural difficulties and inter-personal problems have been in existence before an overdose or act of DSH, the greater the likelihood of a repetition[12, 17]. Among adolescents who deliberately harm themselves, the following factors are most likely to be associated with a higher risk of later suicide:
- Male gender
- Older age
- High suicidal intent
- Psychosis
- Hopelessness
- Unclear reason for the DSH

11.22 The use of a screening questionnaire to predict the degree of risk in adolescent DSH patients may be helpful. Such a questionnaire is set out in Table 13 below. The higher the total score the more DSH should be considered of concern.

Table Thirteen

PATHOS Screening Questionnaire

1. (P)	Have you had <u>P</u>roblems for longer than one month?	
2. (A)	Were you <u>A</u>lone in the house when you overdosed?	
3. (T)	Did you plan the overdose for more than <u>T</u>hree hours?	
4. (HO)	Are you feeling <u>HO</u>peless about the future: that things won't get much better?	
5. (S)	Were you feeling <u>S</u>ad for most of the time before the overdose?	

(Kingsbury, 1993)

11.23 While these approaches provide useful pointers, the extreme complexity involved in any form of prediction should always be borne in mind. Skilled intervention, together with, ideally, a hospital admission, is essential if a full understanding is to be gained of the young person's vulnerability. All school-age teenagers who present with DSH should be admitted for physical and psychiatric assessment, irrespective of their physical state. This is more difficult to achieve with older adolescents who may be sufficiently conscious to exercise their right of self-discharge.

Risk Assessment in Other Situations

11.24 Questions of risk assessment also arise in situations where an individual with no previous suicide history is, for instance, seriously depressed or is talking about or threatening suicide.

11.25 In assessing risk in those who have not committed an act of DSH, there are a number of characteristics which are central. These are the exhaustion of personal resources such as hope and energy, and the breakdown of usual defences, the exhaustion of family resources, a state of intolerable stress and the perception of suicide as a viable solution. An individual with these characteristics may have options to change intolerable conditions, but may lack both the psychological and social resources to do so. Thus impaired, more primitive coping patterns emerge, primarily flight (death by suicide) or fight (suicidal behaviour to affect others). Where these goals can be accomplished there is the serious risk of suicide or self-harm.

11.26 There are a number of common themes which may contribute to the overall degree of risk. It is not possible to allocate a precise weighting to these factors but it is generally agreed that at least one and probably more of them are likely to occur in almost all suicides of young people. These factors are:

---

[12] Hawton et al, 1982.

[17] Kerfoot and McHugh, 1992.

a. **A Negative Personal History**

Negative life events, a significant skills deficit, and inadequate models for coping are all elements of this. Particularly important here are a family history of suicide, exposure to suicidal behaviour in peers or a sibling, and parental psychopathology. Prior DSH behaviour in response to real or anticipated loss is also of note.

b. **Psychopathology**

Evidence of psychiatric symptomatology, or personality attributes such as aggression, low frustration toleration, and impulsivity are significant, especially if such characteristics are exacerbated by significant substance abuse.

c. **Stress**

Under this heading are included environmental or psycho-social events which threaten the adolescent's ability to cope effectively. Often these stressors are anticipated rather than real, but represent unacceptable rejection, humiliation or feared punishment.

d. **Breakdown of Defences**

Evidence of cognitive rigidity, irrationality or thought disturbance would be of significance here.

e. **Social and Interpersonal Isolation and Alienation**

Behavioural withdrawal, or isolation, and the rejection of help or involvement with family, school or community are elements of this.

f. **Self-deprecating Ideation, Depression and Hopelessness**

Feelings of pessimism, worthlessness and hopelessness are all involved here. Negative views of oneself, and death-related or suicidal thoughts may contribute to the overall picture.

g. **Method – Availability, Accessibility and Knowledge**

A key element here is the awareness of, and prior attention to, methods of suicide, and knowledge of the whereabouts of weapons, medication or harmful substances.

11.27 If it is decided that there is a risk of suicide, the level of risk must also be assessed. It is useful to consider this in relation to the following questions:

Table Fourteen

Questions Relating to Suicide Risk in Adolescents

Does this patient have the potential for self-harm?	Here the question has to do with whether the patient presents with one or more risk factors in his or her history or current life experience. For example, is there a family history of suicide, or has the patient been exposed to the suicidal behaviour of a peer?
Might this person possibly harm him or herself?	The possibility of suicide increases substantially where there is evidence that death or suicide is on the individual's mind. Additional factors here are cognitive rigidity, and evidence of social isolation or alienation.
If self-harm is possible, what is the probability of such behaviour, and what are the circumstances, the degree of lethality and imminence involved?	Whether suicidal intent will be acted upon depends on a number of situational factors, including conditions of threat or stress, the availability or accessibility of method, and often a particular trigger or event which has a high level of personal meaning for the individual.
Are there continuing provocative factors?	The individual's living circumstances need to be considered, in particular whether there are any deficits in care and supervision.

The degree of risk is at its highest where an affirmative answer can be given to all four questions. Table 14 is reproduced as Check-List 8 (page 111).

11.28 The approach to risk assessment outlined above is not the only possible one, but it is as thorough and comprehensive as any currently available. While the prediction of suicide will always be a difficult task, there is much to be learnt in this field, and much to be developed through concerted efforts to make this knowledge available. Developing the skills of psychiatrists, nurses, general practitioners, counsellors, teachers, social workers, parents and others, endeavouring to help them recognise and assess suicide risk could pay substantial dividends in reducing suicide rates amongst vulnerable groups of young people. Young people come into contact with a wide range of adults, many of whom have no specific training in mental health issues. **Training initiatives to develop early detection and referral-making skills in those adults who come into contact with vulnerable young people should be a key area for resource investment.**

Involving Families

11.29 Parents of teenagers are often the last group to be seen as a resource, and yet they are, more than any other group of adults, the first line of defence. **More attention should be directed to educating and supporting parents in caring for distressed or troubled adolescents.**

11.30 There are, however, some challenges to the family approach. While other factors, such as the presence of psychiatric disorder, require specific treatment, there are usually issues relating to the family's contribution to the crisis, or their response to it, which will need additional, separate attention. Dysfunctional family relationships or communications may need modification. One common problem affecting the whole subject is the reluctance of families and young people to engage in treatment or sustain attendance for more than a few sessions, usually because of an expressed wish to forget the whole episode. A problem-solving approach (see Chapter 9), applied to the whole

family unit, can be appropriate since it can be brief, and seen to be apposite.

11.31 It is, however, important to bear in mind that, although many issues can be usefully addressed through a family approach, this has to be flexible enough to accommodate an adolescent's occasional, but intense, need for the privacy of individual sessions[18].

11.32 Clinicians need to develop skill in the delivery of short-term, focused interventions. They also need to be knowledgeable about adolescence because the common features of adolescent development, such as rebellion, mood swings and deteriorating communication are a regular part of the litany of complaints brought by parents. Putting current problems into a proper developmental perspective gives parents a model for understanding adolescence and reduces the likelihood of the adolescent's identity revolving entirely around his or her suicidal behaviour. These skills can be taught and the short-term, focused nature of the intervention makes it easier to evaluate. So far, no systematic studies (i.e. using random allocation of sufficient numbers of participants to well-defined interventions) of the efficacy of aftercare for children and adolescents who attempt suicide have been published. The work of Rotheram-Borus et al (1994) in New York, USA, who focus on brief cognitive-behavioural treatment for suicidal adolescents and their families, looks promising, as does the development of a brief home-based intervention for families (Kerfoot et al, 1995).

School-based Interventions

11.33 A number of approaches to intervention based in schools have been tried in recent years. Few of these have been in this country: the majority have been in

---

[18] Kerfoot, 1986.

the USA or Australia and there has also been work in Israel. Given the differences in cultural environment in schools in different countries, it is not easy to translate experience in one country to another, but the work is interesting and worthy of consideration.

11.34 These schemes divide into two types, those that can be described as *educational*, aimed at raising general awareness about suicide and self-harm, and developing skills of risk recognition among pupils and staff[19], and on the other hand those that can be described as *screening*, aimed specifically at preventing further imitative suicides following one or more such incidents in a school[20].

11.35 The former usually involve a course of weekly sessions focusing on attitudes, emotions and awareness of skills for coping with distress. The aim of this approach is to effect substantial changes in inter-personal skills, and in addition, a reduction in suicidal ideation amongst those who take part in the programme. There is some pessimism about the effectiveness of the approach. There is little evidence of a change in attitudes as a result of the approach, perhaps because of the weakness of a didactic educational model in health promotion or possibly because the programmes were insufficiently intensive or not targeted at a high risk group. A less didactic approach, based on cognitive-behavioural modification principles, has shown positive gains in inter-personal skills amongst those who took part. In summary, the way forward would appear to be through continued refinement of screening procedures since the review by Shaffer et al (1988) found little evidence for the success of 'buddying' schemes in schools, or peer group surveillance.

11.36 Turning to the screening approach, several attempts have been made to develop ways of identifying adolescents at risk of suicidal behaviour. Two approaches have been used. In one, pupils at school were educated in risk factors; subsequently, they were expected to persuade friends who were showing signs that indicated they might attempt suicide to seek professional help or, if this seemed unlikely to succeed, to inform an appropriate adult. Unfortunately this did not seem to work as the pupils simply did not take the actions that were hoped for. In the second approach, the pupils themselves were asked to complete a questionnaire which identified risk factors. The problem here seemed to be that, although the questionnaires yielded valid results, the risk factors they identified were so common that too many adolescents were identified – the old problem of false positives.

11.37 There is a further approach, often described as "postvention", which also presents difficulties. Postvention refers to work carried out with a school in which there has been a recent suicide, in order to minimise the chance of imitative suicidal behaviour and to alleviate guilt among others. What is clear is that the ethos and organisation of the school is as important as any professional interventions; the attitudes of staff, and the way that the school as a whole responds to the incident, are critical in determining the pupils' responses. Intervention must be very rapid, must involve a core group of staff who are perceived to be influential in the school, and it must involve as many pupils as possible, rather than focusing only on the immediate peer group of the individual who died. More work is needed in this field but, potentially, it could be of great value to schools in developing their preparedness to cope with traumatic incidents of this type.

---

[19] Klingman & Hochdorf, 1993.

[20] Hazell, 1991.

Services for Adolescents at Risk of Suicide

11.38 Table 15 deals with the components of a comprehensive service for those at risk of suicide. However, in considering services aimed at reducing adolescent suicides, the particular characteristics of the age group need to be borne in mind. First, this is the group least likely to be consulting general practitioners on their health needs. Adolescents visit their GPs less than any other age group, a fact which has significance both for the identification and for the management of individuals who are at risk. Second, once adolescents have left school they are likely to be mobile in respect of housing and to be less in contact with institutions and community services. In particular, those who are most vulnerable may be out of work or may have no stable employment. Such young people may also find it difficult to stay in further education or to stick at job training schemes.

11.39 In evaluating the quality of services available to adolescents, it is important to consider the following:

Table Fifteen

Issues to be Considered in Evaluating the Quality of Services for Adolescents

Is there provision for the full assessment and treatment of a young person who exhibits any of the risk factors for suicide?	This should include provision for those with depressive disorders, those who misuse alcohol or drugs and for those with severe anti-social behaviour. In particular, it is important to identify whether there are professionals who are able to identify depression in young people and treat it vigorously.
Are there local health promotion policies which address the needs of adolescents?	These should include policies targeted at especially vulnerable groups, such as homeless young people and those in the care of the local authority.
Is there provision for the full assessment of a young person following an act of DSH?	It is important to ensure that there is provision for younger adolescents to be admitted overnight to medical wards for observation and interview even when they do not obviously need physical resuscitation. There should be local guidelines that ensure that this happens.
Can the assessment of young people who have been admitted be undertaken in adequate privacy?	This is important if the full background is to be established.
Are there professionals available who have the appropriate training in the assessment of suicide risk and personal safety in adolescents?	Professionals should have the ability to identify psychiatric disorder which requires treatment and should be well informed as to local resources in both the statutory and voluntary sectors. They should be aware of which services and agencies are likely to be most acceptable to this age group.
Do local prescribing policies allow local psychiatrists to prescribe anti-depressants which are minimally toxic in overdose?	It is important to prevent hoarding as far as possible.
Are there local guidelines for the management of young people who harm themselves and are these subject to clinical audit?	Clinical audit protocols and programmes should recognise the specific characteristics of this age group.
Are there sufficient treatment resources for psychiatric disorders and family disturbances which may have been revealed by assessment?	These should include both specialised mental health resources and less intensive but accessible community primary care and counselling services. It is important that these primary care and counselling services are appropriate for young people.
Are there arrangements for suicidal adolescents to be admitted promptly to an appropriate adolescent psychiatric ward or unit?	The unit needs to be sufficiently local to enable other family members to participate in treatment. Each health authority should have a contract with such a specialist unit.
Is there clear evidence of good communication between emergency services (Accident and Emergency or Casualty Departments), adolescent mental health services, general practitioners and, where appropriate, community paediatricians, school doctors, and social services?	There should be adequate liaison between all these groups, which is supported by appropriately flexible relationships based on mutual understanding of the needs of adolescents and young people.

This table is reproduced in Chapter 20 as Check-List 22 (pages 126 and 127).

11.40 Where services already exist, there is a need to consider whether they require strengthening. Resources should be targeted towards improving the skills of all concerned in the field of work with young people with mental health problems. This includes parental education and professional training. Existing primary care and counselling services should be extended to complement the specialist mental health services. The latter can usefully be engaged in providing consultation to, and supervision and training of, primary care workers and counsellors.

11.41 Primary care, counselling services and specialised mental health services need to be seen as being located on different tiers of service. **Counselling is not a substitute for a specialised service, yet it can be more acceptable to a young person or his or her family than specialised services such as those provided by child and adolescent psychiatric clinics or adult community mental health teams.** It therefore has a contribution in cases where severe psychiatric disorder is not present. Counselling may also play a preventative role in personal and inter-personal conflict before a crisis is reached.

11.42 In particular, youth counselling and advice facilities and drop-in centres specifically designed for the adolescent and young adult age group need to be supported and developed in all major population centres. The possibility of providing counselling services located in, or connected with, drop-in centres, colleges, training centres and major employers of young people should be encouraged. There is also a role for the media in promoting public education about adolescent suicide and suicide risk.

11.43 High numbers of cases of DSH amongst young women and increasing rates of completed suicide in young men have lent a special urgency to the task of intervention and prevention. If the Health of the Nation targets are to be met, it is important to build on models of good practice already available. Training at all levels is essential, but a substantial proportion of such training should be targeted at those who are the most likely first to identify risk – parents, general practitioners and teachers.

Chapter Twelve

Suicide and Depression

12.1 Depression can play a very important aetiological role in decisions made by sufferers to commit suicide. Indeed, some kind of depressive state is the most common clinical picture to be found in persons who proceed to kill themselves (though it must be remembered that a significant number do not have these features). Table 16 illustrates the range of symptoms and behaviours reported retrospectively in a representative sample of 100 suicides.[1] In looking to prevent suicide, therefore, it is important to detect and treat depressive symptoms at an early stage. The fact that depression can easily be missed makes those who suffer it a particularly vulnerable group of people.

Table Sixteen

Symptoms of 100 Suicides Recorded in 20% or more of Patients during 4 Weeks Prior to Death

	Depression N = 64 %	Alcoholism N = 15 %	Miscellaneous N = 14 %	Not Mentally Ill N = 7 %	All N = 100 %
Looked miserable	89	40	43	0	69
Insomnia	86	80	50	29	76
Taking hypnotics	70	73	43	29	64
Weight change	69	67	57	57	66
Looked anxious	67	53	43	29	60
Complained of sadness	64	60	14	14	53
Weight loss	61	47	43	43	53
Difficulty in working	61	33	21	0	47
Reduction in work	53	53	43	0	48
Less interest	53	40	29	14	45
Pessimistic or hopeless about future	52	47	21	0	43
Anorexia	50	60	21	0	44
Less social activity	47	27	43	0	40
Less energy	47	33	29	0	39
Slower movements	45	40	43	14	42
Reproached self	44	40	7	14	36
Difficulty in concentrating	42	33	21	0	35
Weeping	42	60	14	14	39
Restless	41	40	14	0	34
Diurnal mood variation	38	20	43	0	30
Hypochondriacal	36	53	7	14	35
Indecisive	33	20	7	0	25
Thought self a burden	33	20	29	14	29
Slower speech	31	40	57	0	34
Thought self useless or worthless	31	33	14	0	27
Thought let people down	28	27	7	0	23
Complained of anxiety	28	40	43	14	31
Trembling/shaking	22	53	14	0	24

[1] Barraclough et al, 1974.

12.2 General practitioners are in the front line in the detection of depression. It has been calculated that a general practitioner will see at least one patient with mild depression or worse at each surgery. In 1991, two consensus meetings between representatives of the Royal College of Psychiatrists and the Royal College of General Practitioners considered the assessment and management of depression in general practice. The recommendations have been summarised elsewhere.[2] Some of the most important points, however, are summarised below:

Table Seventeen

How Common is Depression?

- 5% of the general population at any one time may be suffering from major depression.

- 3% of the general population are diagnosed by GPs in a year as suffering from depression.

- 3 per 1,000 of the general population are referred to psychiatrists in a year because of depression.

The main reasons why depression may be missed can also be summarised:

- Depression may occur secondary to physical illness.
- Depression may present with somatic complaints.
- There is reduced insight in the patient.

- Ethnic minority background.
- Elderly people.

} because overt depression is thought, erroneously, to be less common in this group.

The clinical features of major depression are set out in Table 18. It is important to identify depression at an early stage when it may be less severe, and the rigid criteria set out in the Table

should not prevent this. This material in the table is taken from the DSMIIIR classification.[3] The recently published ICD10 guidelines, though based on a similar clinical descriptive approach, utilise the terminology *depressive episodes; mild; moderate; or severe (with or without psychotic symptoms).*

Table Eighteen

A summary of DSMIII-R criteria for major depression

At least five of the following symptoms present during the same two-week period. This must include at least one of the symptoms of depressed mood and diminished interest or pleasure.

1. Depressed mood.
2. Markedly diminished interest or pleasure in normal activities.
3. Significant weight loss or gain.
4. Insomnia or hypersomnia.
5. Agitated or retarded.
6. Fatigue or loss of energy.
7. Feelings of worthlessness or excessive guilt.
8. Diminished ability to think or concentrate, or indecisiveness.
9. Recurrent thoughts of death or suicidal thoughts or actions.

NB. No evidence of other primary disorder

12.3 Other forms of depression important in general practice include depressive episodes which do not reach the threshold for major depression and lifelong mild fluctuating depression with dysthymia. Manic-depressive illness (bipolar depression) is less common.

12.4 The Consensus Meeting encouraged an active treatment policy based on symptoms themselves, making the point that a decision as to whether the illness is 'endogenous' or 'reactive' can be unhelpful. Drug therapy, such as antidepressant medication, can be useful even when a 'reactive' mechanism is considered to be significant. The treatment approach should always be broad-based, addressing a multi-factorial set of causal factors: it is a safe axiom to

[2] Paykel and Priest, 1992.
[3] American Psychiatric Association, 1987.

assume that every instance of depression is both endogenous and reactive in nature.

12.5 There is considerable current debate on the role of the various types of anti-depressant drug in the management of depressed people. The older tricyclic drugs, with the risk of cardiovascular complications which can be very serious in overdose, are being challenged by new, selective serotonin re-uptake inhibitors and reversible monoamine oxidase-A inhibitors which, though relatively free from side-effects and less likely to be toxic in overdose, are at present very new to the clinical scene. Whatever group of anti-depressants is used, there should be scrupulous prescribing practice, that is, careful control of the quantities prescribed at any one time, if necessary eliciting the help of relatives to take responsibility for the safe-keeping of drugs, in order to reduce the risk of hoarding.

12.6 In the treatment of depression, a judicious, differential use of the various types of anti-depressant drugs according to type of clinical picture and individual responsiveness is of undoubted importance. However, some important problems in the drug management of persons who actually proceed to commit suicide have long been identified. One study has shown, for example, that only half of the people who commit suicide whilst depressed had been treated with anti-depressants, and many had received long-term medication in doses too low to be effective.[1]

12.7 **In reaching out and listening to suicidal individuals, skills specifically relevant to depression are very important.** Although it is useful to reassure a depressed individual, great care should be taken not to reassure excessively. Reassurance too liberally given can be taken to signify that the professional person has failed to understand and has underestimated the depths of despair the individual feels, which may then be accentuated. The precise experience and meaning of depression can be difficult to explain, and it may not be easy for patients to express the full extent of the distress that they feel. Depression implies a loss of emotional reactivity to the sufferer's personal environment and towards others. Things that are normally enjoyed may accentuate this awful sense of separateness and loss of feeling. It is often useful, at interview, to ask a person whether he or she feels different from the normal self, ie from the way he or she usually feels, and to explain that it may not be easy to put this into words.

12.8 Hopelessness is a very common theme. There may be an inability even to construe the future. It is always important to ask about morbid (abnormal and excessive) self-blame, particularly so if major depression is suspected. Delusional ideas of self-blame are easily missed and the severe impairment of judgement which has earned the title psychosis may go undetected in severe depression. Such a patient may even seek to discontinue contact with a health care professional. Whenever a patient with depression says that he or she does not think he or she should continue to attend, it is always important to clarify the reason behind this statement. He or she may, of course, be better, but occasionally the situation is a dangerous one, because, in some instances, those people who are suffering continuing severe depression with self-blame may be trying to assess the professional's conviction that it is worthwhile for them to go on with life. Patients in this situation may be suici-

---

[1] Barraclough et al, 1974.

dal and testing out opinion before finally deciding to commit suicide.

12.9 It is in instances of depression, too, especially with regard to persons whose condition has failed to respond to treatment or in whom the disorder has relapsed recurrently, that professionals are liable to adopt negative attitudes to the extent that they become judgemental and critical in the face of the apparently inexplicable failure to respond to repeated overtures of help. Such a situation occasionally develops into one of malignant alienation in which the sufferer becomes progressively isolated from help. Such a sequence of events can be important in leading to the final scenario which ends in suicide. Prevention of this situation requires careful evaluation of the circumstances when a person appears to be failing to respond to treatment. Professional teams should have procedures which allow for objective review.

12.10 This is not to deny that some patients need limits to their behaviour to be set. Situations of this kind may present significant challenges in developing treatment plans to help patients to relinquish their maladaptive ways of trying to cope. However, staff in mental health services should be aware that this is by no means always the case. Indeed, professionals sometimes fail to appreciate how disabled a depressed patient really is and expect too much, in their

efforts not only to get that patient well, but to do so rapidly. The quiet inward suffering of depression is all too easily misconstrued.

12.11 The physical and somatic aspects of depressive illness must also be remembered. This not only applies to the physiological changes of insomnia, anorexia and weight-loss; complaints of physical illness and physical symptoms can, in themselves, be important ways in which depression presents. In major depression, hypochondriacal fears can be bizarre and sometimes delusional in their intensity. The need to assess mood and to search for depressive illness, as a complication of fully established organic disease, should be borne in mind as depression is a related and important aspect of organic illness.

12.12 In childhood and adolescence, depression may well be missed because clinicians are either not convinced that an illness of this kind can occur in young people, or because they are wrong in assuming that symptoms such as mood disturbance, loss of interest, or even weight-loss are reactions to the normal developmental challenges and demands of adolescence. There is a need for assessors to take special care in interviewing young people, and for them to modify their interview style to enable children and adolescents to give a full account of their worries and feelings in their own words.

Chapter Thirteen

Suicide Amongst Prisoners

13.1 Suicide among prisoners has increased considerably over the last ten years and at a rate higher than that in the general population.[1] **Rates are three to four times higher than in the general population.** As a sub-group, prisoners have distinctive characteristics relevant to suicide risk and need to be given special consideration. Furthermore, within this sub-group, young offenders constitute a discrete group requiring particular attention (see paras 13.6 and 13.7 below).

The Distinctive Characteristics of Prisoners who Commit Suicide

13.2 A number of stresses, specific to the prison situation, appear to be associated with, and probably contribute to, suicidal behaviour.[2] These include the prospect of a long-term imprisonment, inability of individuals to cope with confinement or the prison regime and the fear of intimidation or victimisation within prison. The lack of communication with the outside world is also significant, especially the threat to close relationships, for example, through divorce or separation, or by the family ostracising the prisoner. Receiving bad news concerning domestic problems or, perhaps, the failure of an appeal can also be important, as is guilt about the offence.

13.3 The average age of people in prison who commit suicide is in the mid-30s – an age which is slightly higher than the average for the prison population as a whole. The highest risk period is early in a prison sentence with approximate-

ly one in six suicides occurring in the first week of incarceration and approximately one in two in the first three months. Remand prisoners are at particular risk. The rate of suicide is greater in prisoners convicted of murder and for those convicted of violent or sexual crimes. Suicide risk is also greater in prisoners serving longer sentences. However, it is important to remember that, while many suicides occur during the early part of a period of imprisonment, some prisoners see prison as a form of asylum and they may find release a threatening prospect. Suicidal ideation may result from this fear among prisoners who are approaching the end of their sentences.

13.4 Although not as close as in the general population, the association of psychiatric illness with suicide does exist with regard to prisoners. Of those prisoners who commit suicide, approximately one in three has a history of previous psychiatric illness and one in four has had an admission to a psychiatric unit. One in three has a history of alcohol abuse, while one in five has abused drugs. Almost one in two has a history of deliberate self-harm (DSH) and half of these people have harmed themselves during their current prison sentence, although the method of DSH is rarely the same as that used in eventual suicide. Almost one in four has received psychotropic medication in the month prior to suicide and one in two has seen the prison doctor in the week prior to his or her suicide. (About one in three prison suicides occurs whilst the prisoner is in the prison hospital). Only

---

[1] Liebling, 1993.　　　　　　　[2] Dooley, 1990.

one in six prisoners who commit suicide is noted as being at risk, but one in two has been regarded as 'manipulative' or 'attention-seeking'. The application of these many risk factors to prediction of risk in individuals is, as in clinical practice in a wider setting, limited because of their low specificity and low sensitivity which leads to the identification of many false positives and false negatives.

13.5 A proportionately higher number of prison suicides appear to occur between midnight and 8am. It also appears that prison suicide rates peak during the autumn, which is in sharp contradistinction to the overall pattern of suicides in which the frequency peaks during the spring. The reasons for this difference are not clear.

Young Offenders

13.6 Young men aged 15-24 are six times more likely to kill themselves in prison than their peers outside. Some young offenders have a marked vulnerability to DSH and suicide. People in this group are likely to have backgrounds of emotional deprivation and to show an inability to cope with, or make constructive use of, their time in prison. They have little contact with their families and make few friends and have more difficulties relating to other inmates. In general, they experience prison as particularly distressing. It appears that it is the combined effects of hopelessness, their previous life experience, their current situations, and their inability to generate any solutions to their problems that propel these young prisoners towards suicide.

13.7 While some studies show that a violent offender profile is associated with suicide risk in young offenders, others do not. More consistent is the finding that

a higher than expected number of suicides occur among remand prisoners and amongst those who are at an early stage of their custody – that is, during what is probably the most stressful stage of custody. Factors contributing to risk may include the tension and uncertainty of the pre-trial phase, the proximity of the offence, overcrowding, staff shortages and the instability of a constantly changing inmate population. One other factor may be the number of remand prisoners placed in custody far from their homes, making visiting especially difficult. Links with family and partners are highly significant protective factors for young men at this stressful time. Almost half of suicides in young offenders have been attributed to 'prison pressures'. Within the prison population as a whole, young prisoners, especially those under 21, represent the largest group of individuals at risk.

Preventative Measures Specific to Prison

13.8 A number of key factors need to be addressed in considering suicide prevention in prison. In certain circumstances, prisoners experience gross overcrowding and this may well be a factor leading to an increased suicide rate. Rates might be reduced if periods of remand were to be shortened and transfers to psychiatric hospital, when appropriate, were made without lengthy delays. All staff members should have adequate training in the psychological care of prisoners and, in particular, the assessment and management of suicidal prisoners. Improvements in the rapport and trust between staff and prisoners is likely to foster suicide prevention. The recent innovation which has made the Samaritans' process of befriending available to prisoners is a most welcome development. HM Prison Service has recently embarked upon an enlightened training programme for its staff, one which emphasises assessment and support which includes psychosocial as well as medical and psychiatric approaches.

13.9 Suicide risk should always be considered in planning the design and regime of a prison, in order to minimise the means of committing suicide. Given the preponderance of hangings amongst prisoners who commit suicide, it is important to ensure that, for example, the prison environment presents as few opportunities for this method as possible. If a prisoner is considered at risk of suicide, it is sensible to undertake a thorough search for possible dangerous objects (such as belts, wires, ties). Similarly, vigilance should be high during the times of highest risk, both for the general population of prisoners (at night, in the autumn) and for individual prisoners (at the beginning and at the end of their time in prison). Staff should also be aware that behaviour which may be described as manipulative or attention-seeking is also associated with an increased risk of suicide.

Chapter Fourteen
Non-Fatal Deliberate Self-Harm

14.1 The link between non-fatal deliberate self-harm (DSH, parasuicide, attempted suicide) has already been discussed in Chapter 3 (paras 3.12 and 3.13). This is not the place for a comprehensive review of the management of DSH (there are excellent texts available for reference[1]). In June 1994, the Royal College of Psychiatrists published The General Hospital Management of Adult Deliberate Self-Harm – A Consensus Statement on Standards for Service Provision which included particular reference to the management of patients who present to Accident and Emergency Departments following an episode of DSH. DSH in adolescents is dealt with in Chapter 11 (paras 11.8 to 11.23).

14.2 All patients who deliberately harm themselves should be offered a full psychosocial assessment. In some services, this task is shared between professional groups. Where this is the case, the supervision and training of those who conduct these assessments must be of a high standard and the service should be part of a co-ordinated scheme. An important point to remember is that the degree of medical harm in DSH may bear little relationship to the degree of psychological disturbance. The aim must be to identify whether there are suicide and other relevant risk factors present, and if so, to determine their significance.

14.3 While it is possible to discern risk factors which correlate statistically with suicide at some later date, these are of such low specificity and sensitivity that some have dismissed the risk factor approach in trying to prevent suicide. This is

unjustified. Risk factors are useful, if only as a double-check on clinical assessments. Their presence in a patient who is judged to be free from suicide risk should, at least, require the clinician to ask him or herself whether the evaluation is correct and prompt him or her to review the situation again before allowing such a patient to go home.

14.4 The assessment should be comprehensive and should cover all the points set out below. These are replicated in Check-List 6 (pages 107 and 108).

Table Nineteen

Psychiatric Assessment of DSH Patients

A. HISTORY

1. Brief History of the DSH event
   a. what were the precipitating events?
   b. what were the motives for the act?
   c. what were the circumstances of the act?
   d. were any precautions taken against discovery?
   e. were there any preparatory acts, eg procuring means, putting affairs in order, warning statements or suicide note?
   f. how violent was the method?
   g. how lethal (potentially) were the drugs or poison used?
   h. had there been symptoms of depression, such as listlessness or social withdrawal, preceding the act?
   i. is there any sign of the use or abuse of alcohol (which is a depressant and also a disinhibitor)?

2. General Psychiatric and Medical History
   a. have there been any previous acts of DSH?
   b. what was the nature of any previous psychiatric disorder?
   c. if any, how was it treated (as in or outpatient, by GP, with drugs or with what other treatment)?
   d. is there a family history of depression or other psychiatric disorder, suicide or alcoholism?
   e. is there evidence of present or previous physical illness?

3. Social Circumstances
   a. housing – does the patient live alone?
   b. does the patient have a job?
   c. what is the reaction of family and friends to the act of DSH?
   d. who will take the patient home and look after him or her?

Continued overleaf

[1] Hawton & Catalan, 1987.

e. family attitudes are relevant – what needs to change, are relatives likely to sympathise, can they be involved in therapy?

f. the quality of family relations – is there any evidence of physical, sexual or emotional abuse, if a teenager?

g. is there a social worker or a probation officer involved with the patient?

h. are difficulties likely to worsen or improve following the act of DSH?

4. Background

a. is there any relevant family and personal history?

b. is there an extended history of excessive drinking or drug abuse?

c. is there a premorbid personality problem or disorder?

d. if the patient has a criminal record, what are the details of that record, including periods in prison, on remand, on probation or in any other offender institution?

B. MENTAL STATE (Points for Particular Attention)

a. consider whether the patient is of dejected appearance, agitated, restless or depressed.

b. ask, specifically, whether the patient is depressed on waking and whether the mood lifts during the day (ie diurnal variation).

c. does the patient have impaired sleep (difficulty in getting off to sleep, frequent or early morning waking)?

d. is the patient experiencing feelings of guilt, unworthiness, or self-blame?

e. is the patient suffering impaired appetite with weight loss?

f. are others incorporated into the patient's nihilistic ideas?

g. ask specifically about suicidal thoughts and intentions.

h. is the patient pessimistic about his or her ability to resume – and cope with – normal life?

i. is another psychiatric syndrome present? (DSH is associated with a wide range of disorders, eg schizophrenia, substance abuse, personality disorders, organic brain syndrome and epilepsy.)

C. FORMULATION

a. why the overdose was taken or episode of DSH committed.

b. psychiatric diagnosis (illness and personality). There may be no psychiatric disorder.

c. assessment of risk of suicide or non-fatal repetition after recovery from DSH, bearing in mind the risk factors present. Address risk to others (for example, dependent children).

d. problem areas (to be defined with the patient) bearing on further care.

e. action to be taken – establish goals.

(With acknowledgements to R Gardner,[2] on whose work it is based)

14.5 There are also factors associated with a higher risk of repetition of DSH[3] and these include:

- problems with the use of alcohol;
- diagnosis of psychopathy;
- previous psychiatric inpatient treatment;
- previous psychiatric outpatient treatment;
- not living with relatives.

14.6 Although overnight inpatient admission after DSH has long been traditional policy, increasingly patients who attend because of DSH tend to be discharged home directly from the Accident and Emergency (A and E) Department and in some centres up to 30% of cases are dealt with in this way. This may be related to a shortage of inpatient beds. In such circumstances, every effort should be made to ensure that an adequate psychosocial assessment has been made before the patient leaves. People who attend A and E Departments following superficial self-inflicted skin lacerations are especially likely to be managed in this way. It has already been mentioned that the degree of physical risk in DSH may not be a reliable guide to the severity of psychological distress. It is, therefore, important to ensure that adequate psychosocial assessments are offered to **all DSH** patients who attend Accident and Emergency Departments. In the case of childen and school-age adolescents, inpatient admission is usually essential.

14.7 Communication between hospital doctors and general practitioners must be rapid and effective. A telephone call is best, but, in any case, the psychiatrist should ensure that his or her recommendation is sent as part of the house physician's discharge letter immediately the patient is discharged. A subsequent further letter is also advisable giving the full psychiatric and social assessment. This should not be so delayed that it arrives too late to be part of the urgent, effective and well-coordinated action by everybody concerned.

---

[2] Gardner, R., 1991.

[3] Buglass & Horton, 1974.

14.8 In some cases the patient will need to be followed up by the Mental Illness Services. The principles of the Care Programme Approach apply just as much to DSH patients as to others. The assessing doctor should ensure that rapid communication occurs with anyone who has already been identified as the key worker. DSH patients show a poor compliance with help offered to them. Only about half attend the psychiatric outpatient clinic appointments to which they have agreed at the time of hospital admission. While this may be due to rapid resolution of the crisis, making subsequent treatment seem irrelevant to the person who self-harmed, or may reflect a reluctance to discuss personal problems, it can also be the result of deficiencies in the way help is offered. **The way psychiatric help is presented to patients is crucial – it must be seen to be relevant to the problems faced by each patient.** Since mental illness commonly reduces insight adequate treatment is essential. When the patient is able to cope with the challenges involved, a problem-solving approach (see also Chapter 9) can be very helpful.

14.9 It has been suggested[4] that a service which reaches out to persons after episodes of DSH through offering help at times of crisis rather than at fixed appointments can reduce the frequency of non-fatal repetition. The Green Card approach offers help in this way provided the person has not actually repeated an act of deliberate self-harm. Table 20 reproduces the information which was given to patients as part of this study. (This is reproduced as Check-List 9 (page 112)).

In future developments of this approach it may not be feasible to offer overnight admission in such a forth-

right way, given the massive reduction of inpatient resources in recent years. Nevertheless, the principle and spirit of the Green Card can still be maintained by offers of immediate availability of help at all times, with strong discouragement of repetition of self-harm.

Table Twenty

The Green Card
(used following DSH)

Instructions on how to use this Card

This card explains how to get immediate help from the hospital if, in the future, you feel despairing, unable to cope or have thoughts of harming yourself.

At any time of the day or night, a doctor in psychiatry is available to speak to you on the phone, or see you in person at the hospital.

The doctor will discuss your problem with you and tell you how he or she can help. If you would like a break from home to help put your problem in perspective, the doctor will arrange for you to stay on one of our wards overnight.

Important

You must contact the doctor on duty **instead** of harming yourself if he or she is to help you.

If you have **already** harmed yourself (eg by an overdose), the doctor will have to refer you straight to the Casualty Department. This is because you may have put your physical health at risk.

Keep this card on you, eg in your wallet or handbag. If you do lose it, you can get a replacement from your GP.

If you need help, either –

1. **Telephone** the number on the front of this card and ask for extension XXX (this will put you through to a unit at the hospital).

2. Ask to speak to the **nurse in charge.**

3. Say that you have a **green card** and would like to speak to the **doctor on duty.** (You need not give your name if you don't want to).

4. The nurse will take your number and ask the doctor to phone you back as soon as possible.

or:

1. **Go in person** to the **Accident and Emergency Department** of the hospital.

2. Show the last page of this card to the **receptionist** and say that you would like to see the **doctor on duty.**

3. The receptionist will show you where you can wait, and will call the doctor for you.

It is already clear that the Green Card approach, if it is to work effectively, should not be used indiscriminately.

---

[4] Morgan et al, 1993.

Some patients abuse it, leading to considerable stress on the participating staff. Any Green Card System needs to include adequate supportive supervision for staff who provide the telephone cover. It is also advisable to allow for the exclusion of a small number of patients who already have demonstrated a tendency towards violence, perhaps specifically to staff, or inability to accept guidance, particularly involving the abuse of alcohol.

14.10 Assessment and management of DSH patients demand all the clinical skills described in the previous chapters. Concomitant problems associated with episodes of DSH, particularly the degree of risk for others, such as dependants or children, require very careful assessment in addition to the assessment of risk of suicide or non-fatal repetition on the part of the patient.

PART D

THE IMPLICATIONS FOR COMMISSIONING

AND PROVIDER MANAGERS

Chapter Fifteen

Characteristics of a Good Comprehensive Mental Illness Service

15.1 Whatever the setting, the essential principles of good clinical practice in relation to suicidal individuals can be clearly defined. The following draws together points from previous chapters and refers to the whole of the care network from general practitioners and primary health care teams through specialist community mental health services to hospital in-patient facilities. It includes items which should be evaluated in any effective clinical audit procedure (see Chapter 17). Provision of training for professionals (psychiatrists, nurses, psychologists, occupational therapists, social workers and other local authority staff) and continuing medical education are important matters which merit separate consideration in Chapter 16.

Philosophy of Care

15.2 The approach of a service to suicide prevention should be clearly understood by staff at all levels. Positive attitudes to suicide prevention should be encouraged and negative attitudes, when detected, should be addressed. There should be recognition of the need for a range of interventions to be offered, including psychological, social and physical interventions and treatments. The need to involve relatives and key others in both the assessment and management of suicide risk should be acknowledged as should each individual's rights and autonomy. There should be an appropriate balance of medical and psycho-social models in the management of each individual and a readiness to use both hospital and community components of the service.

The aims of the service should be understood by all those working within it and appropriate training should be available to promote that understanding and improve skills. The use, and regular updating, of codes of practice in both hospital and community, particularly with regard to supportive observation techniques, and good communications involving effective links between all components of the service, are essential. The Care Programme Approach is now a standard way of ensuring that all who are concerned with a patient's care meet regularly with the identified key worker.

Clinical Skills

15.3 Skilled interviewing is vital to the assessment of suicide risk and those working in this field should have adequate interview training. They need also to be skilful in assessing the degree of suicide risk and aware of the hazards to be negotiated during clinical assessment. The use of well-defined supportive observation procedures in hospital ought to be well understood as should the problems of prescribing medication, particularly with regard to drugs which are potentially toxic in overdose. Regular training in basic resuscitation procedures should be provided.

The Availability and Accessibility of Services

15.4 The accessibility of the service to its users and the image it projects are important. Access points and the ways in which contact is facilitated can influence the willingness of those at risk both to make contact and to maintain that contact once made. Drop-in access can be a valuable form of help for suicidal persons. Assertive outreach to known at-risk groups who are unlikely to initiate contact themselves is essential, as is collaboration with voluntary organisations such as the Samaritans. It can be helpful for hospital or other specialist staff to act as consultants to such organisations and there should certainly be provision for advisory links. A good service will act in alliance with others, for example, social services departments, the probation and prison services, and will have good working relations with them.

15.5 Availability is not just a question of access to the service by users. The different components of the service have to be available for advice and support to each other. There need to be clearly defined mechanisms for community consultation with primary health care teams on both urgent and non-urgent bases and effective links between community and hospital-based services to ensure good continuity of care. For example, there should be adequate support available in the community for patients during the high risk period following discharge from hospital and, similarly, hospital staff should be available for domiciliary assessment.

Community Services

15.6 Issues of availability have a considerable influence on the extent to which suicide risk can be managed in the community. Services should have clear operational guidelines, devised in the light of local circumstances, with regard to the assessment and management of persons in the community who are at risk of suicide. These should include the degree of severity beyond which this type of care is no longer

appropriate or practicable. Good community care requires not only psychiatric knowledge and skills on the part of the practitioner but, crucially, also an ability to commit time, and this should be reflected in the locally-agreed guidelines.

Psychiatric Inpatient Facilities

15.7 The provision of beds in psychiatric units should be sufficient to allow the ready admission of persons at suicide risk as necessary. It should also allow for the need to avoid premature discharge when patients may be showing misleading clinical improvement without the whole range of problems having been addressed effectively. There should be provision of a milieu in the inpatient unit which is free from excessive levels of disturbance and which suicidal patients will see as non-threatening and supportive. Important too is an awareness of the needs of long-stay patients, especially when ward changes or closures are being implemented. Staff should recognise the need to assess those at risk on an individual as well as a group basis.

15.8 On the ward, facilities should be available to allow intensive care of persons at high risk of suicide, as necessary. These include adequate provision of numbers of staff and physical security, as appropriate. Physical hazards in the ward should be checked regularly. The number of medical and nursing staff needs to be adequate to cover 24 hours of the day, weekends, Bank Holidays and times of staff changeover. One, or more, key workers should be readily available to each patient.

Other Hospital Facilities

15.9 It is important to ensure adequate provision for the urgent specialist assessment and management of people at risk of suicide and of other patients attending Accident and Emergency Departments and elsewhere. Clear procedures regarding both admission and discharge of such patients are essential. There should be provision for the admission of young adolescents to appropriate paediatric or adolescent medical wards and contractual arrangements for prompt admissions to an inpatient adolescent psychiatric unit whenever this is indicated following assessment. These facilities, and the arrangements for psychiatric liaison services, may well involve more than one provider service and commissioning authorities should ensure that co-ordination between services is achieved. Non-psychiatric staff who may come into contact with people at risk of suicide need to receive training in dealing with such cases and to have available specialist advice and support. Audit of ward hazards should be carried out regularly.

Support for Bereaved People

15.10 All staff should have appropriate skills in the basic techniques involved in helping people who suffer bereavement after suicide. Relatives and key others who are bereaved in this way are liable to experience special problems over and above the normal bereavement process and staff should possess appropriate clinical skills, for example with regard to breaking bad news and dealing with the special hazards experienced by this group of people.

Special at Risk Groups

15.11 Certain groups of people should be given special consideration in the provision of services in view of their acknowledged higher risk of suicide. The provision of specific codes of practice may be appropriate. Such groups

include those who have deliberately harmed themselves, elderly people, particularly persons in community residential facilities, those with problems of alcohol or substance abuse, severely mentally ill people, especially those in the community with psychotic illness, and adolescents. There may be other specific groups, depending on location, including for example, city centre and rural homeless people, farmers and ethnic minority persons. In each case, the pattern of service provision and the awareness of the specific problems of each group should be reviewed to ensure that provision is sufficiently sensitive to their needs.

Communication

15.12 It is important to ensure that all relevant information is both sought and documented, so that no important factor is missed. Full documentation means that all those in contact with persons at risk of suicide have all the information they need to make decisions on risk and management. A good service will have adequate mechanisms for record-keeping and communication at, and between, all levels of the service. Only in this way will those at greatest risk be identified and their needs addressed. The Care Programme Approach is now a standard way of ensuring that all those who are concerned with the care of a patient meet regularly with the identified key worker.

15.13 Table 21 overleaf summarises the points made in the preceding paragraphs. Read in conjunction with Table 15 on page 60 (Checklist 22 on pages 126 and 127) on services for adolescents, it indicates what should be considered in evaluating the quality of services provided for those at risk of suicide.

Table Twenty One

**Issues to be Considered in Evaluating the Quality of Services for
Persons at Risk of Suicide**

Is the philosophy of care appropriate and understood by all concerned?	The aims of the service should be understood by all working in it. Positive attitudes to suicide prevention should be encouraged and negative attitudes addressed. The role of relatives and key others in both assessment and management should be recognised, and at the same time, the rights and autonomy of the individual acknowledged.
Is there a balanced range of interventions available?	These should include psychological, social, and physical treatments, in community and hospital settings.
Do staff possess the necessary skills and is there provision for updating these skills as appropriate?	Skilled interview techniques are vital. The procedures for well-defined supportive observation should be thoroughly understood, as should the effect of drugs both in terms of side-effects which may affect the patient's mood, and toxicity in overdose. Regular training in basic resuscitation should be available and there should be provision for on-going training and education for all staff.
Are staffing levels adequate?	There should be sufficient trained staff available at all times, including weekends, holidays and times of staff changeover. More specialist help should be available as required, especially to those staff working in the community.
Does the service make itself available to those who need its help?	A good service acts in alliance with other agencies, such as social services departments, the Prison Service and voluntary bodies such as the Samaritans, and will have good working relations with them, offering advice and support. It will reach out to those at greater risk.
Are there clear operational guidelines for community-based care?	Guidelines should be readily available in each unit and fully understood by all persons involved in patient care.
	These should include a clear indication of the degree of severity of risk beyond which this type of treatment is neither practicable not appropriate.
Can those working in the community commit the necessary time to the task?	This is vital to good community based services. Where sufficient time cannot be committed, other approaches should be considered. The time commitment should be covered in operational guidelines on community-based care.

Chapter Sixteen

Training

16.1 Training is a key issue. It is difficult to evaluate the effects of training, but they are implicit in the work of knowledgeable and skilled staff and in the efficient and effective working of services. When services are running well and functioning at an optimal level, the contribution of training is taken for granted and easily forgotten. When things go wrong, however, training (or the lack of it) is often cited as one of the root causes of failure. So, in addressing the reduction in the rates of suicide, it is also necessary to consider issues of training.

16.2 Crisis intervention is too often regarded as no more than one part of the repertoire of professional people, rather than being worthy of particular attention. The idea that some special knowledge and skill is necessary to work with crisis situations has declined in importance in recent years and has accompanied the decline of deliberate self-harm (DSH) as a specialism for nurses, social workers and others. In this way, ignorance and mis-management may be perpetuated through the erroneous belief that suicidal behaviour requires routine, rather than specialist, intervention.

16.3 In truth, effective intervention with people expressing suicidal ideas and behaviour requires particular skills. The development, and maintenance, of these skills requires thorough training and a commitment to continuing education. Furthermore, work with people in crisis, those under stress and those at risk of DSH and suicide is, in itself, extremely demanding, not to say stressful. Staff, therefore, need access to support and supervision as a routine part of their work if they are not to become de-skilled, cynical or, worse still, incapacitated themselves. Thus, the training task has both general and specific applications. In the general sense, basic knowledge and skills regarding suicidal behaviour and its assessment and management should be incorporated into professional training at the qualifying level for GPs, social workers, nurses and psychologists. This level of training should be substantial enough to enable all trainees to make an assessment of a suicidal person, and for them to be able to formulate a management plan. Since most professional training requires its trainees to undertake periods of supervised practice, it should be possible to ensure that they have exposure to patients with suicidal behaviour and opportunities to put what they have learned into practice.

16.4 Training has specific applications for those whose main area of work is in the mental health field, and in other scenarios where their patients may be particularly vulnerable. For these staff a co-ordinated training programme is needed. This should include a more in-depth and sustained training approach, so that core knowledge and skills are consolidated, development is available through refresher training and the whole enterprise is underpinned by regular supervision. Supervision and consultation provide an opportunity for front-line workers to take their learning forward. Their work experience becomes a vehicle for teaching and other colleagues can contribute and gain insight.

16.5 Within this continuing learning context, periodic top-up teaching is likely to have a far greater impact than an isolated short course or series of one-off lectures. It also means that team members are active partners in the learning process rather than passive recipients.

16.6 The basic principles of care for suicidal people, including first aid and resuscitation, should be made part of student nurse training very early in their ward attachment, and this should ideally involve the ward medical staff. Facilities for resuscitation should be readily available and their location known to all staff.

16.7 Junior doctors, too, should receive instruction in the care of suicidal people at the earliest possible time following their entry into psychiatric training. Their seniors should emphasise the principle that good care depends on the fullest possible communication between nurses and doctors on a regular basis.

16.8 Staff training and education should challenge negative attitudes such as the assumption that suicide is inevitable in certain patients or that individuals have at all times a right to end their lives. They should be taught to avoid any hostile rejection of their patients or a personal conviction that suicide prevention is not relevant to the care of certain individuals.

16.9 It is important that all staff develop this positive approach to dealing with suicidal people. Only then will they utilise to the full their specific knowledge and skills. The core knowledge and skills should cover all the points listed below. The table is reproduced as Check-List 15 (page 118).

Table Twenty Two

Core Knowledge and Skills
• Basic knowledge of psychiatric conditions, particularly the many presentations of depressive illness and more minor conditions.
• Models of suicidal behaviour, antecedents, process and prognosis.
• Monitoring and assessment, with particular reference to severity and risk.
• Methodologies for responding to an emergency.
• The professional and personal resources needed in managing crises.
• Therapeutic interventions including brief, focused work, and the indications for longer-term involvement.
• Multidisciplinary working, managing conflict in attitudes, opinions and beliefs.
• The role of voluntary agencies in monitoring and support.

16.10 **It is important that all staff, from whatever discipline, who have contact with suicidal people, understand the principles of good care**. This goes well beyond those staff who work exclusively in the mental health services. The need for training for social workers and psychologists has been referred to above, but they are not the only groups. Staff on medical wards and in Accident and Emergency Departments, who have the care of patients after an act of DSH have a particular need to understand the care of suicidal people. So also have prison staff and those working for voluntary and non-statutory organisations, such as the Samaritans.

16.11 Within the NHS, managers in particular require this understanding as the procedures involved in good care have significant personnel management, staff training and supervision, staff welfare and resource implications. **In-service training of managers should include basic clinical matters to ensure that they understand the principles on which patterns of care are based. It is vital that managers understand the stress and strain to which professional staff are exposed as this should have an important impact on their understanding of the need for training and support services.**

Chapter Seventeen

Clinical Audit

17.1 Clinical audit is essentially a review of clinical practice, carried out in such a way that various deficiencies in clinical procedures are identified and, where possible, remedied. It can have particular benefits in the case of suicide and its prevention. Research in this field is beset with difficulties, with the result that the clinical assessment of suicide risk is still a very uncertain matter; the at-risk factors which have been identified are notoriously unreliable, especially in the short-term. Given this situation, it is very important that the day-to-day clinical procedures in the assessment and management of suicide risk are identified and locally agreed. This is exactly what clinical audit can do. **Clinical audit, properly conducted, may lead to the identification of a new range of short-term predictive factors, hitherto uncharted by conventional research.** The whole process should enable and encourage health care professionals to look at what they do, thereby energising their will to achieve excellence in clinical practice.

17.2 It is important to acknowledge that not all suicides, given the present state of knowledge, can be prevented, however good the clinical service. The purpose of clinical audit is, quite simply, to optimise clinical practice so that preventable suicides are avoided. The review needs to be systematic and comprehensive and ideally should involve the use of a standardised questionnaire to include all aspects of the problem; otherwise the process tends to be selective, excluding difficult issues and perhaps merely leading to mutual reassur-

ance. The relevance of such audits to suicide in persons who have received some form of care is obvious. But the significant proportion of people who commit suicide and who have not been in contact with services also needs to be reviewed and this should, ideally, have the primary health care team taking the lead.

17.3 The simplest approach is to review those unexpected deaths which become known to health care personnel. However, any clinical audit which sets out to be comprehensive must also match local mortality data (including that from HM Coroner's inquests) with the records of those who have used any component of the mental health service. These records include those of hospital inpatient facilities, community mental health teams, day hospitals and outpatient facilities. General practitioner surgeries must also be included in a comprehensive review. An efficient matching process depends upon the reliability of all sources of data. The process may appear cumbersome but it is essential to collect and match data in this way because hospital-based practitioners can be unaware of some unexpected deaths in patients within a year of discharge from their care. This means that lessons learned in hospital practice from day-to-day clinical experience in the assessment and management of suicidal individuals may be unreliable. Effective audit is a mechanism to help rectify this.

17.4 Detailed guidelines concerning clinical audit into unexpected deaths are now available.[1] The process is inexpensive

[1] Morgan, 1994.

and can easily be developed under normal working conditions, without the need for extra resources. It is, however, a challenging task requiring co-ordination and persistence, and it can be very helpful to identify a special audit co-ordinator who can ensure that mortality data are collected, disseminated, and checked with all components of the clinical service, and then considered by regular audit meetings. Audit should be multidisciplinary in nature. A questionnaire such as that used in the Confidential Enquiry into Unexpected Deaths is a helpful mechanism for ensuring that all aspects of the problem are reviewed. The same questionnaire can then be used for returns both to the national Enquiry and for the purposes of local audit.

17.5 **Clinical audit should encourage clinicians to learn from shared experience based on reliable case register data, rather than aim at finding scapegoats or apportioning blame.** It is essentially a process whereby what is learnt from experience is regularly built into codes of clinical practice. Fears of medico-legal repercussions can inhibit enthusiasm but such anxieties can be allayed by ensuring that documentation is in the form of lessons to be learnt together with actions to be taken, without reference in detail to individuals or named instances of suicide which have been reviewed. Clinical audit will never succeed if it is confused with enquiries into clinical practice which managers may need to conduct under complaints, or other, procedures.

17.6 When such enquiries take place, it is of the utmost importance that they are conducted with sensitivity and an awareness of the many difficulties faced by professionals in negotiating the hazards which can arise in caring for persons at risk of suicide. It is far too easy, with hindsight, to see deficiencies in any clinical service. Such enquiries need to identify problems which ought to be rectified, but criticism which is insensitive and, perhaps, unfair in the circumstances can do much damage to clinical confidence, producing defensive practice which can then become less effective in preventing suicide.

17.7 In view of the difficulties which beset the day-to-day care of suicidal persons, **the accumulation of lessons learnt through reliable clinical audit is a vital part of any service which sets out to be as effective as possible in suicide prevention.** Clinical audit is not merely a way of implementing the lessons learned from more formal research; it can itself identify new ways of understanding the many pathways which lead to suicide. Improving the process of care is an important theme in its own right and is one approach to the challenging task of suicide prevention.

Chapter Eighteen

The Implications for Commissioners

18.1 In bringing together current knowledge, theory and practice into a guide that serves to inform those charged with assessing and managing suicide risk, the previous chapters are primarily an aid for those providing mental health services. The framework of the NHS and social services, however, requires the shared commitment of both providers and commissioners, whether Health Authorities (HAs), Family Health Services Authorities (FHSAs) or General Practitioner (GP) Fundholders or Local Authority Social Services Departments (SSDs). Indeed, it is the commissioners, with their responsibilities for improving the health of their respective populations, who will be held accountable for progress made towards the targets set by the Health of the Nation initiatives. The key issues for commissioners are set out in Table 23 below (which is reproduced as Check-List 16 in Chapter 20 (page 119)). These address the direct role of commissioning in the prevention of suicide, and follow the 'seven stepping stones' approach to effective commissioning.

Strategy

18.2 NHS procedures on setting and management of performance focus strongly on a short-term annual cycle. The Health of the Nation strategy recognises the need for a longer-term view in handling complex health and health outcome-related work. Commissioners need to establish a long-term approach to suicide prevention. This approach, which should involve a framework based on short- and medium-term action contributing to a long-term goal, should not, however, be incompatible with an annual performance management cycle. Indeed commissioners may concentrate on immediate gains by focusing on high risk groups or areas. This, in itself, can have benefits in reducing scepticism about the feasibility of suicide prevention, by demonstrating progress and making early contributions to the ultimate target. Immediate actions pursued individually or jointly with providers might include those cited in Table 24. This is reproduced in Chapter 20 as Check-List 17 (page 120).

Table Twenty Three

Key elements underpinning good commissioning

- Strategy

- Effectiveness through contracting

- Developing the knowledge base

- Responsiveness to the population

- Partnerships with providers

- Healthy alliances

- Organisational fitness, ie improving the skills and attitudes of managers

Table Twenty Four

Strategic Measures Which Purchasers Might Take

Measures to improve quality and efficiency of Services
- Establish multidisciplinary audit meetings on suicide and DSH.

- Establish or contribute to local prison suicide prevention groups.

- Ensuring through contracts, new, or improved, observation policies on key wards.

- Establish a district or locality-based suicide prevention group.

- Ensure that all providers with whom they contract are implementing the care programme approach and supervision registers.

continued overleaf

Measures to promote prevention and early intervention services

- Commission a specialist aftercare service for people who deliberately harm themselves.

- Encourage providers to prioritise training for all staff dealing with people who deliberately harm themselves or are at high risk of suicide.

- Produce specialist information and support to vulnerable occupational groups, such as farmers.

- Ensure that arrangements exist for the prompt and sensitive assessment of adolescents who deliberately harm themselves.

- Establish a database for data collection on vulnerable groups of people.

Where there is sufficient evidence from locally-gathered information, initiatives may be focused on locally-derived priority groups as well as those vulnerable groups of people identified by national statistics. Success in these smaller performance areas can serve to demonstrate short-term progress whilst contributing to the longer-term – three to five year – target or change in trend. **All initiatives require close monitoring to record progress and their impact on specific suicide rates in different groups of people.**

Effectiveness Through Contracting

18.3   In the past, many contracts have been concerned mainly with increasing the volume and reducing the unit cost of services, regardless of their effectiveness. Commissioners need to place effectiveness – which has been described as the science of doing the right things – at least on the same level as efficiency. They should use contracts to change the structure of provision to increase health gains. Although the unit cost may be high, some therapeutic services offer greater health gains. This should be borne in mind when contracting and commissioners should not be constrained by a tradition of support for a particular service or technique where these are shown to be ineffective.

18.4   **It is through the medium of contracting, contract monitoring and service**

review that commissioners have the potential to influence the effectiveness of services for suicide prevention. Contracts for mental health services should specify the elements set out in Table 25 below. This is reproduced in Chapter 20 as Check-List 19 (page 122).

Table Twenty Five

- Full implementation of the care programme approach as well as monitoring and reporting arrangements.
- The maintenance and development of a mental health information system, including supervision registers.
- Staff adequately trained in the care programme approach and in risk assessment and management.
- Suitable arrangements for the management and clinical supervision of staff in community mental health teams.
- Audit of suicides.
- Agreed procedures in the event of a homicide or assault by a patient subject to the care programme approach.
- An agreed statement or protocol describing how suicidal adolescents will receive inpatient care.

The above list forms a basis upon which commissioners could superimpose specific local issues highlighted by audits undertaken locally.

18.5   Check-Lists 21 (pages 124 and 125) and 22 (pages 126 and 127) provide both service commissioners and providers with items they might consider for discussion in their review meetings. Checklist 21 is presented in Chapter 15 as Table 21 and Checklist 22 appears in Chapter 11 as Table 15.

18.6   The skills of identifying suicide risk and of effective management described in previous chapters may well require additional training and resource input. Inevitably, these will be subject to local negotiation but commissioners should recognise that a simple contract currency of a finished consultant episode (FCE) may be insufficient to address the full range of what is required.

18.7   It should not be forgotten that a large element of the work undertaken by non-statutory agencies contributes to the prevention of suicide, both in the general population and amongst specific groups (eg Samaritans, Relate, Cruse, MIND, National Schizophrenia Fellowship). Many of these agencies contribute significantly to the community support network that helps people in times of crisis and vulnerability. Contractual relationships with these organisations are often ill-defined and open to the vagaries of the local financial situation. Commissioners should, however, recognise the effectiveness (and cost-effectiveness) of these services and should reflect this in their approach to contracting with them by seeking to secure more permanent and focused relationships with the non-statutory sector.

18.8 When contracting with non-statutory organisations, commissioners need to develop a framework that is simple and facilitates the delivery of performance which meets the expectations of the commissioners, both in terms of activity and quality. It should also create stability in the non-statutory organisations without inhibiting the flexibility traditionally offered by such non-statutory providers. The contracts between non-statutory bodies and NHS commissioners should not preclude the providers from continuing to attract resources from elsewhere. Many non-statutory providers receive funds from local authorities and joint commissioning approaches can prove valuable. A number of options are available:

a. **Option One: Core Contracting**
An exercise to identify the key non-statutory providers in relation to the local purchasing strategy should be carried out. Each key organisation is then offered a rolling service agreement to provide the minimum element of the service required to ensure its existence year on year. This might, for example, involve meeting the salary and on-costs of a service co-ordinator, the costs of administrative support or the payment of rent and, if applicable, council taxes. On occasions, it can be appropriate for the premises to be

provided. There may be, in addition, a need for a small operational budget to cover volunteer staff expenses. Any further costs are then to be found by the organisation itself, perhaps from charitable income, trust funds or one-off grants. A useful benefit of this approach is the ability of the commissioner to maintain confidence in the financial framework governing the income and expenditure of smaller, more vulnerable non-statutory services.

b. **Option Two: Sub-Contracting**
This involves negotiating a block contract with a local non-statutory umbrella organisation such as the Council for Voluntary Services. The organisation is required to grant-aid or contract with a range of providers operating in specified service areas. While commissioners lose some direct contact with their providers, they gain from not having to perform management functions for a large range of small contracts with individual non-statutory organisations.

c. **Option Three: Selective Contracting**
This approach involves identifying the strongest non-statutory providers (ie those with strong local ties, solid management structures or national profiles) and negotiating their delivery of services in key areas. Within the framework, commissioners can negotiate service agreements which utilise the full range of contractual options. Collection of evidence to support contracts (activity data and performance indicators) should be the responsibility of the providers and it is often valuable to encourage the development of audit mechanisms as a tool for ensuring quality.

The key points in the above are summarised below in Table 26.

Table Twenty Six

Options for Consulting with Non-statutory Organisations

Option 1 — *Core* Contracting

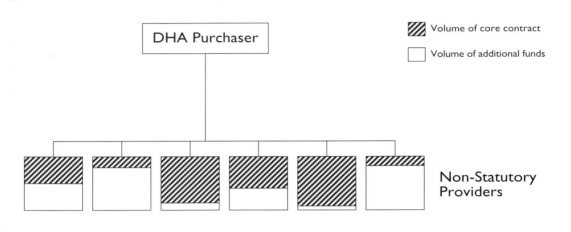

Option 2 — *Sub*-Contracting

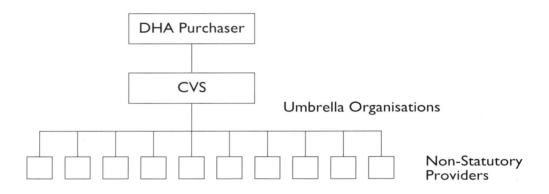

Option 3 — *Selective* Contracting

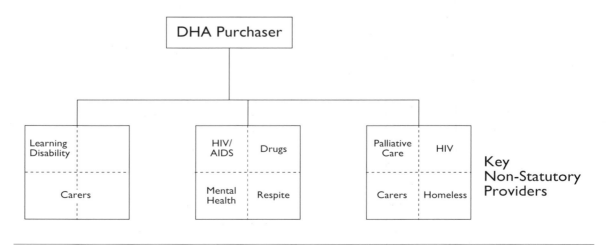

18.9 Current practice in relation to contracting with the non-statutory sector is variable geographically and in terms of subject area and between agencies. **In order to secure the involvement of key services that may be required to achieve targets, it is essential that a consistent approach, through the development of a purchasing framework, is achieved.**

Developing the Knowledge Base

18.10 It is clear that a rapid development of the knowledge base for commissioning underpins its ability to bring about health gains. Previous chapters provide an extremely valuable resumé of current knowledge on suicide prevention, with the key concepts summarised in Chapter 19. The bibliography also offers an important set of references, for further reading. Thorough briefing provides a broad base to influence directly the development of services.

18.11 The required knowledge base for commissioners has been defined[1] in Table 27 below, and is reproduced in Chapter 20 as Check-List 18 (page 121).

Table Twenty Seven

The Required Knowledge Base for Commissioners

- Resource allocation.

- Quality management and resources.

- Appropriate outcome measures.

- Evaluating different approaches to contracting.

- Population-based health assessment.

- Methodology for priority setting.

- Cost-effectiveness of services.

- Cost-effectiveness of interventions.

18.12 In the light of this, it is apparent that there are significant gaps in the existing knowledge base in relation to suicide prevention specifically, and as

regards mental health services generally. It is, therefore, important that commissioners seek to set early local objectives for improving their knowledge base. These might include establishing local suicide rates and specific local risk factors and the interrogation of databases, such as Coroner's records. It would also be useful to establish an explicit profile of current spend on areas related to suicide prevention, such as that on the care programme approach, contracts with the relevant statutory agencies, contracts with the non-statutory sector, the follow-up of DSH cases, and the spend on people with a severe mental illness, as well as on GP counselling schemes. Undertaking prospective local research or contributing to broader research projects into suicide risk and the effectiveness of on-going suicide prevention initiatives can also provide useful information.

Responsiveness to Populations

18.13 The recent NHS reforms have increased the importance of commissioners responding to their local populations. This role is more complex than simply asking local populations to help identify local health priorities. In essence, the relationship between commissioners and their populations involves seeking a mandate from the population for spending on suicide prevention at a time when many people are sceptical about the effectiveness of suicide prevention. This, in itself, requires the dissemination of information in order to facilitate and inform public debate. The vulnerability of at-risk groups needs to be highlighted in order to involve the public in suicide prevention. Stimulating a local debate can engender a stronger sense of community aimed at reducing isolation and offering vulnerable individuals more

[1] Research for Health, Department of Health, 1993.

support. Commissioners should also seek to engage the local population in the local assessment of need and share with it the outcome of current suicide prevention approaches in order to maintain momentum and validate spending in this area. However, in developing this level of public involvement, it is important for commissioners to avoid reinforcing stereotypes and the stigma that can be associated with mental health problems.

18.14 Many commissioners, in addressing issues such as these in other fields, have already begun to develop new skills for engaging with the public, through using the local media, publishing details of services available in local resource directories, developing new relationships with Community Health Councils (CHCs), involving users and carers in service planning, offering financial support for self-help schemes, and stimulating user-led lobbying groups, amongst other activities. All of these approaches can have value in suicide prevention.

Partnership with Providers

18.15 While the relationship with providers is essentially defined through contracting, it should be acknowledged that contracting is a technical function and its real impact can be enhanced or reduced as a result of the general context of the relationship between each commissioner and each provider. The successful prevention of any avoidable death is clearly the common goal of both partners in relation to suicide prevention. A successful partnership engenders the sharing of expertise in improving the mental health status of populations, the effective targeting of resources aimed at suicide prevention and the avoidance of the unnecessary waste of resources used to rectify disagreement and mistrust. Whilst most

of this is well understood, it highlights the need for joint commitment. A number of relationships within the partnership will be worthy of particular investment, if the joint objective is to be achieved.

18.16 The role of various elements in the partnership is set out in tabular form in Table 28 below.

Table Twenty Eight

Chairman, Chief Executives, Senior Executives and non-Executive Directors
- set appropriate policy directives.
- provide key messages (eg that suicide can be prevented).
- model the partnership climate for all the organisation.

FHSA Medical Advisors, public health commissioners together with key providing professionals
- agree local priorities on suicide prevention.
- negotiate, and then monitor progress against targets and performance measures.
- share expertise on suicide prevention.
- ensure effective targeting of resources in health gain areas.

Planning Officers
- liaise on resourcing priority areas.
- set the service context for preventing suicide.
- liaise on the provision of key data and information to enable monitoring.

The nature and qualities of these partnerships and of the relationships within the purchaser-provider system rely on the continuing commitment of staff at all levels in both purchaser and provider organisations and highlights the need for collaboration outside the formal joint bodies and committees.

Healthy Alliances

18.17 **Working across agency and disciplinary boundaries is a necessity for commissioners if they are to improve the health of their populations.** For many organisations, however, the concept is tarnished by unfortunate previous experience. Such misgivings are likely to be based on experience of large, unwieldy and ineffective bureaucracy, characterised by financial disagreements, mistrust of other professions and, at its worst, disbelief in the ability and competence of partner agencies. But the nature of suicide prevention presents commissioners with tasks that can only be achieved through healthy alliances. In the light of previous (and possibly unsuccessful) experience, there is now a better understanding of the basic principles for achieving success in inter-agency working. These include:

Table Twenty Nine

- an understanding that collaboration is a means to an end, namely improved quality and outcome for service users.
- shared values and principles between organisations (or an understanding and recognition of where these differ to enable negotiation).
- structural mechanisms that are set within a context of informal networking and relationships.
- a planning process that reflects the priorities of the senior levels of management and couples them to the working experience of staff at the grassroots of the organisations.
- an agreed language that allows honest discussion of different positions rather than tokenistic acceptance of superficial ideology.
- clear specification of the task and the timescale within which it will be achieved.
- appropriate and committed representation that is empowered to take decisions or reflect the decision making process of the organisation.
- access, if possible, to a joint or jointly committed budget.

These principles are reproduced in Checklist 20 (page 123) for ease of reference.

18.18 In relation to suicide prevention, a number of alliances can prove useful to commissioners. The list given in Table 30 is illustrative and is not intended to be either prescriptive or comprehensive. Commissioners may find other partnerships appropriate in their particular locality and in the light of their specific population needs.

18.19 Before leaving the subject of healthy alliances, it is perhaps worth a note of caution. While it is possible to envisage a wide variety of alliances which could have an added value in suicide prevention, it is well to bear in mind that it is the quality not the quantity of alliances that is of paramount importance.

Table Thirty

Examples of Inter-Agency Partnership

Partnership Agency for Commissioner	Potential Key Tasks of the Partnership
Local Authority a. Social Services	• Implementation of community care reforms, including the care programme approach, development of comprehensive services post reprovision of long stay hospitals. • Effective needs assessment.
Local Authority b. Environmental Health	• Organising a DUMP campaign for unused medication.
Local Authority c. Education Service	• Development of good system of pastoral care (which might include counselling offered by school nurses). • Offering education on suicide and deliberate self-harm. • Strategic deployment of detached youth workers.
Prisons (also police staff involved in custody arrangements in local stations)	• The reduction of suicide in prisons through effective treatment or transfer of mentally disordered offenders. • Improving the assessment and management of suicide risk by prison staff.
Samaritans (and other voluntary organisations such as Relate, CAB etc)	• Ensuring effective support for individuals at vulnerable times such as marital breakdown, bereavement, debt.
Non-Statutory Alcohol and Drug Counselling Services	• Ensuring effective support for individuals with alcohol and drug problems exhibiting suicidal behaviour.
DSS, Job Centres, and Job Clubs	• Ensuring vulnerable individuals are not socially isolated and remain in contact with neighbours etc.
Probation Service	• Identifying and supporting individuals at risk within its caseload.
NHS Trusts	• Ensuring effective management and treatment of those at risk of suicide. • Providing training and role support to other partner agencies. • Implementing the care programme approach and supervision registers.

Organisational Fitness: Improving the Skills and Attitudes of Managers

18.20 Negative attitudes to suicide prevention do not exist solely amongst professionals. Commissioners too may have negative attitudes and may find it illuminating to test their views against those set out in Check-List 2 (page 103). Equally, if faced with scepticism on the part of mental health providers, where the knowledge base on suicide prevention is stronger, it may be difficult for commissioners to challenge negative attitudes. In such circumstances, there is a tendency to accept scepticism and this may be reflected in commissioners' own strategic decisions. It is, therefore, important for commissioners to develop access to expertise that provides a strong understanding of suicide prevention and to use this to take the local debate forward.

18.21 The model set out below in Table 31, which is based on an idea of K Tones, explores this further[2]. The model reveals that attitudes and beliefs held by commissioners can contribute to their ultimate commissioning decisions. The responsibility of all commissioners is to increase their knowledge base, explore and consider the actions being taken by other commissioners and to be prepared, in the light of this, to appraise or re-appraise their own attitudes. A positive attitude towards the task promotes effective and motivated decisions on resource allocation and organisational effort.

Table Thirty One

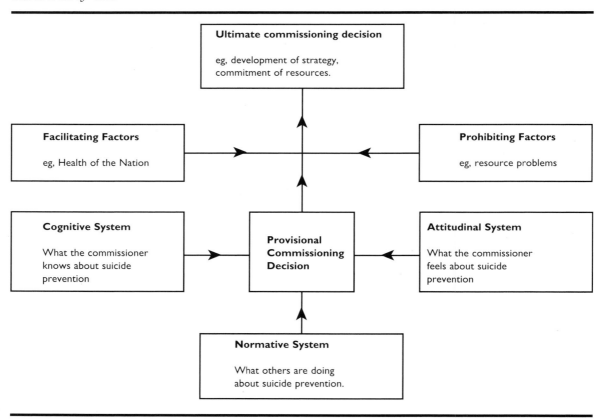

[2] Tones and Tilford, 1994.

18.22 Commissioners should not be deflected from the broad task of improving the mental health of their populations by a narrow debate on the value of national or local suicide targets. **Suicide prevention is a fundamental element of a comprehensive and effective mental health service and that must be the requirement of all commissioners.**

PART E

SUMMARIES

AND

CHECK-LISTS

Chapter Nineteen

A Summary of Key Concepts

19.1 The objective of the Health of the Nation mental illness key area is that of reducing ill-health and death caused by mental illness (paragraph 1.4).

19.2 Suicide is not always preventable but sound clinical practice can help to avert it in certain clinical situations (paragraph 2.1).

19.3 Suicide is one of the major causes of death, accounting for 1% of all deaths annually (paragraph 3.2).

19.4 Since it is likely that many suicides are recorded as 'undetermined' deaths, the suicide rate is probably even higher than it appears (paragraph 3.2).

19.5 Suicides by men outnumber those by women by a ratio of more than 2:1 (paragraph 3.3).

19.6 The increasing suicide rates amongst young males give cause for concern, having increased by 75% in the 15-24 year old age group since 1982, but the highest suicide rates are still found amongst elderly people, in particular those over 75 (paragraph 3.3).

19.7 It is vital to assume that change for the better is always possible (para. 4.1).

19.8 There should be no reservations about the task of suicide prevention (paragraph 4.4).

19.9 The principles of care inherent in suicide prevention relate to the whole spectrum of clinical psychiatric and mental health service practice (paragraph 4.4).

19.10 The belief that it is feasible to prevent at least some suicides should permeate all those concerned with the treatment of a suicidal individual whether in hospital or in the community (paragraph 4.8).

19.11 Risk factors are correlates and associates, and not necessarily causes of suicide. They are more effective in predicting risk in the long-term rather than the immediate future (paragraph 5.1).

19.12 The final evaluation of risk must depend upon individual clinical assessment and that must take into account the differential weightings of risk factors in each person (paragraph 5.2).

19.13 Suicide risk in any individual can only be assessed effectively by full clinical evaluation consisting of a thorough review of the history and present illness, assessment of mental state and then a diagnostic formulation (paragraph 5.3).

19.14 Assessment of risk must depend primarily upon a thorough and comprehensive evaluation of the total clinical picture in each case (paragraph 5.9).

19.15 Risk factors can represent an important element in routine clinical assessment. They are particularly useful as a 'double check', suggesting caution if risk is judged to be trivial yet risk factors are prominent (paragraph 5.9).

19.16 Interview technique should aim to bridge the gap created by mistrust, despair and loss of hope that anything can change for the better (para. 6.1).

19.17 To reach out and listen is itself the first major step in reducing the level of suicidal despair (paragraph 6.2).

19.18 Treatment begins when contact is made, preferably by procedures which reach out to persons at risk and encourage them to seek help at an early stage (paragraph 7.3).

19.19 The basis of good practice, wherever it is based, is the formation of a supportive understanding relationship with the patient (paragraph 7.5).

19.20 Community management is not appropriate when suicide risk escalates beyond a critical level and there are significant limits in supporting mechanisms (paragraph 7.8).

19.21 Management in the community is appropriate where the suicidal intent of the person is judged to be manageable in that setting and there is a good rapport with the patient (paragraph 7.9).

19.22 Implicit in a decision to manage a patient in the community is the principle that the person retains the greatest possible responsibility for his or her own actions (paragraph 7.11).

19.23 Grounds for caution should prompt a review of management (paragraph 7.13).

19.24 A written contract negotiated between the therapist and the patient can be a useful technique in suicide prevention (paragraph 7.14).

19.25 Suicide in psychiatric hospitals has become an important clinical problem which demands careful evaluation of present-day clinical practice (paragraph 8.1).

19.26 A guaranteed, minimum, agreed level of staffing is essential (paragraph 8.8).

19.27 Intensive levels of supervision should depend on the appropriate provision of staff, rather than impersonal physical barriers (paragraph 8.8).

19.28 The appropriate level of supportive observation should be decided as a result of discussion between medical and nursing staff (paragraph 8.14).

19.29 Normally, the level of supportive observation should not be relaxed without joint medical and nursing consultation. It may be intensified, if judged necessary at any time, by the nursing staff unilaterally, should the doctor not be immediately available for consultation (paragraph 8.14).

19.30 Supportive observation should be seen as a therapeutic plan rather than custodial care (paragraph 8.15).

19.31 It must be remembered that suicide risk is only one aspect of any clinical problem. Other potential risks, such as aggressive behaviour, should also be evaluated and managed, in order to ensure safety of other patients as well as staff (paragraph 8.15).

19.32 Throughout the period of care, clear documentation and communication are essential to provide a universally understood and well co-ordinated approach (paragraph 8.28).

19.33 The first few weeks after discharge represent a period of greatly increased risk of suicide (paragraph 8.38).

19.34 A problem-solving approach can be very useful, particularly in facilitating other strategies and is not in any way exclusive (paragraph 9.3).

19.35 Focusing on drug and alcohol abuse would have a greater impact on adolescent suicide rates than any other primary prevention programme (paragraph 11.6b).

19.36 Follow-up studies of teenagers who take overdoses show that up to 11% will die by their own hand over the next few years (paragraph 11.10).

19.37 Training initiatives to develop early detection and referral-making skills in those adults who come into contact with vulnerable young people should be a key area for resource investment (paragraph 11.28).

19.38 More attention should be directed to educating and supporting parents in caring for distressed or troubled adolescents (paragraph 11.29).

19.39 Counselling is not a substitute for a specialised service, yet it can be more acceptable to a young person or his or her family than specialised services such as those provided by child and adolescent psychiatric clinics or adult community mental health teams (paragraph 11.41).

19.40 In reaching out and listening to suicidal individuals skills specifically relevant to depression are very important (paragraph 12.7).

19.41 Suicide rates in prison are three to four times higher than in the general population (paragraph 13.1).

19.42 The way psychiatric help is presented to patients is crucial – it must be seen to be relevant to the problems faced by each patient (paragraph 14.8).

19.43 It is important that all staff, from whatever discipline, who have contact with suicidal people, understand the principles of good care (para. 16.10).

19.44 In-service training of managers should include basic clinical matters to ensure that they understand the principles on which patterns of care are based. It is vital that managers understand the stress and strain to which professional staff are exposed as this should have an important impact on their understanding of the need for training and support services (paragraph 16.11).

19.45 Clinical audit, properly conducted, may lead to the identification of a new range of short-term predictive factors, hitherto uncharted by conventional research (paragraph 17.1).

19.46 Clinical audit should encourage clinicians to learn from shared experience based on reliable case register data, rather than aim at finding scapegoats or apportioning blame (paragraph 17.5).

19.47 The accumulation of lessons learnt through reliable clinical audit is a vital part of any service which sets out to be as effective as possible in suicide prevention (paragraph 17.7).

19.48 All initiatives require close monitoring to record progress and their impact on specific suicide rates in different groups of people (paragraph 18.2).

19.49 It is through the medium of contracting, contract monitoring and service review that commissioners have the potential to influence the effectiveness of services for suicide prevention (paragraph 18.4).

19.50 In order to secure the involvement of key services that may be required to achieve targets, it is essential that a consistent approach, through the development of a purchasing framework, is achieved (paragraph 18.9).

19.51 Working across agency and disciplinary boundaries is a necessity for commissioners if they are to improve the health of their populations (paragraph 18.17).

19.52 Suicide prevention is a fundamental element in a comprehensive and effective mental health service and that must be the requirement of all commissioners (paragraph 18.22).

Chapter Twenty
Useful Check-Lists

This chapter brings together for ease of reference the various summaries and check-lists mentioned in the text. Many of the check-lists repeat material in the individual chapters but, by reproducing them here, it is hoped they will be readily accessible for day-to-day use in clinical practice and in training.

CHECK-LIST 1

The Health of the Nation Mental Illness Key Area Targets
and
The Welsh Health Planning Forum – Protocol for Investment in Health Gain
– Mental Health

To improve significantly the Health and Social functioning of mentally ill people.

To reduce the overall suicide rate by at least 15% by the year 2000 (from 11.1 per 100,000 population in 1990 to no more than 9.4)

To reduce the suicide rate of severely mentally ill people by at least 33% by the year 2000 (from the estimate of 15% in 1990 to no more than 10%).

These figures represent suicide and self-inflicted injury (ICD E950-959) and injury undetermined whether accidentally or purposely inflicted (ICD 980-989).

(Chapter 1, paragraph 1.4)

To increase the proportion of those with a severe mental illness who have a permanent home with appropriate levels of support to 75% by 1997 and 90% by 2002.

To reduce the overall suicide rate by at least 15% by the year 2002 (baseline 1991: males 13.7 and females 3.6 per 100,000 population).

To reduce the suicide rate of severely mentally ill people by at least 33% by the year 2002.

(Chapter 1, paragraph 1.5)

CHECK-LIST 2

Some Negative Attitudes
to Suicide Prevention

1. Suicide is a matter which should be left for the individual to decide.

2. A suicide prevention campaign merely accentuates the guilt of professionals without justification.

3. The causes of suicide in the main are unrelated to medicine.

4. Suicide is a rare event. Clinical techniques are not sufficiently sophisticated for the task.

5. Focusing on suicidal ideas at interview increases the risk.

6. Suicidal individuals do not in any case make contact with professional services.

7. Even when they make contact, they do not declare their suicidal intent.

8. Persons who talk about their suicidal ideas rarely go on to kill themselves.

9. Attention may well become focused on men at the expense of women.

10. Without special training it is best to leave assessment of risk to experts.

11. Increasing risks of litigation make it hazardous to participate in formal reviews of unexpected deaths.

Strongly Disagree ☐
On Balance Disagree ☐
Not Inclined Either Way ☐
On Balance Agree ☐
Strongly Agree ☐

(Chapter 4, paragraph 4.2)

CHECK-LIST 3

How to Interview A Suicidal Patient

1. Ensure that the setting is quiet and minimise the risk of interruption.

2. Do not hurry.

3. Initiate the interview with non-directive open questioning, allowing ventilation of issues and feelings important to the patient.

4. Use language that is appropriate for the patient, take account of variation in cultural values and religious beliefs.

5. Build up trust and rapport quickly.

6. Avoid a brusque, challenging, judgemental approach.

7. Listen to what the patient says.

8. Allow repetitive discussion of issues, if necessary.

9. Take note of non-verbal behaviour that may be of significance regarding suicide risk.

10. Evaluate recent events.

11. Evaluate the patient's mental state.

12. Arrange a physical examination if organic disease is suspected (and routinely in full psychiatric assessment).

13. Beware of the hazards in assessment.

14. Evaluate suicidal motivation carefully.

15. Consider the use of an appropriate risk questionnaire.

(Chapter 6, paragraph 6.1)

CHECK-LIST 4

A Sequence of Questions Useful in Assessing Suicide Risk

Questioning should be open-ended.

These questions are designed to help discover whether the patient:
a. Hopes that things will turn out well.
b. Gets pleasure out of life.
c. Feels hopeful from day to day.
d. Feels able to face each day.
e. Sees a point in it all.
f. Ever despairs about things.
g. Feels that it is impossible to face the next day.
h. Feels life to be a burden.
i. Wishes it would all end.
j. Knows why he or she feels this way (eg wants to be with a dead person, life is bleak, morbid guilt).
k. Has thoughts of ending life; if so, how persistently?
l. Has thoughts about the possible method of suicide (is the means readily available?).
m. Has ever acted on any suicidal thoughts or intentions.
n. Feels able to resist any suicidal thoughts or intentions; and has any thoughts about what would make them disappear.

The interviewer must then consider:

a. How likely the individual is to kill self.
b. The ability of the individual to give reassurance about safety (eg until next appointment).
c. The circumstances likely to make things worse.
d. The willingness of the subject to turn for help if a crisis occurs.
e. Risks to others.

(Chapter 6, paragraph 6.4)

CHECK-LIST 5

Difficulties in Interviewing and Assessing Suicidal People

a. Theoretical: • Base rate of suicide low.   • Difficulty in applying statistically derived risk factors to individuals.   • Short-term versus long-term risk.
b. Practical: • Deliberate denial of suicidal ideas. (Deeply intent on killing self, may appear calm).   • Variability in degree of distress (ambivalence towards suicide).   • Misleading signs of improvement (removed from stress factors yet problems remain unresolved).   • Anger, resentment.   • Unco-operative and difficult behaviour.   • Malignant alienation (deteriorating relationships with others).
c. False Assumptions on the Interviewer's Part: • Assumes that suicidal ideas which are openly admitted are manipulative threats rather than indicative of serious risk.   • Avoids direct discussion of suicidal ideas for fear of encouraging the patient to entertain these.
d. Other Complicating Factors: • Difficulty in deciding degree to which patient should be regarded as responsible for own behaviour, eg setting limits in the case of personality disorder.   • Unpredictable influence of alcohol or drugs.   • Surveillance difficulties.   • Physical hazards in hospital ward or home surroundings.   • Other confounding factors (eg patient a member of EXIT).   • Poorly planned rehabilitation (over-ambitious goals may foster sense of failure).

(Chapter 6, paragraph 6.7)

CHECK-LIST 6

Psychiatric Assessment of the Person who deliberately Harms Him or Herself

A. HISTORY

1. Brief History of the DSH event

    a. what were the precipitating events?

    b. what were the motives for the act?

    c. what were the circumstances of the act?

    d. were any precautions taken against discovery?

    e. were there any preparatory acts eg procuring means, putting affairs in order, warning statements or suicide note?

    f. how violent was the method?

    g. how lethal (potentially) were the drugs or poison used?

    h. had there been symptoms of depression, such as listlessness or social withdrawal, preceding the act?

    i. is there any sign of the use or abuse of alcohol (which is a depressant and also a disinhibitor)?

2. General Psychiatric and Medical History

    a. have there been any previous acts of DSH?

    b. what was the nature of any previous psychiatric disorder?

    c. if any, how was it treated (as in or outpatient, by GP, with drugs or with what other treatment)?

    d. is there a family history of depression or other psychiatric disorder, suicide or alcoholism?

    e. is there evidence of present or previous physical illness?

3. Social Circumstances

    a. housing – does the patient live alone?

    b. does the patient have a job?

    c. what is the reaction of family and friends to the act of DSH?

    d. who will take the patient home and look after him or her?

    e. family attitudes are relevant – what needs to change, are relatives likely to sympathise, can they be involved in therapy?

    f. the quality of family relations – is there any evidence of physical, sexual or emotional abuse, if a teenager?

    g. is there a social worker or a probation officer involved with the patient?

    h. are difficulties likely to worsen or improve following the act of DSH?

4. Background

    a. is there any relevant family and personal history?

    b. is there an extended history of excessive drinking or drug abuse?

    c. is there a premorbid personality problem or disorder?

    d. if the patient has a criminal record, what are the details of that record, including periods in prison, on remand, on probation or in any other offender institution?

B.	**MENTAL STATE**
	(Points for Particular Attention)

a.	consider whether the patient is of dejected appearance, agitated, restless or depressed.
b.	ask, specifically, whether the patient is depressed on waking and whether the mood lifts during the day (ie diurnal variation).
c.	does the patient have impaired sleep (difficulty in getting off to sleep, frequent or early morning waking)?
d.	is the patient experiencing feelings of guilt, unworthiness, or self-blame?
e.	is the patient suffering impaired appetite with weight loss?
f.	are others incorporated into the patient's nihilistic ideas?
g.	ask specifically about suicidal thoughts and intentions.
h.	is the patient pessimistic about his or her ability to resume – and cope with – normal life?
i.	is another psychiatric syndrome present? (DSH is associated with a wide range of disorders, eg schizophrenia, substance abuse, personality disorders, organic brain syndrome and epilepsy.)

C.	**FORMULATION**
a.	why the overdose was taken or episode of DSH committed.
b.	psychiatric diagnosis (illness and personality). There may be no psychiatric disorder.
c.	assessment of risk of suicide or non-fatal repetition after recovery from DSH, bearing in mind the risk factors present. Address risk to others (for example, dependent children).
d.	problem areas (to be defined with the patient) bearing on further care.
e.	action to be taken – establish goals.

(Chapter 14, paragraph 14.4)

CHECK-LIST 7

Assessment of DSH
(Children and Adolescents)

Key Areas in Assessment	
Circumstances of the episode of DSH	• method used • source of agent • availability • likelihood of discovery • suicidal communications • motives • precipitants • previous acts of DSH
Social life and activities	• network of relationships • out of school activities • casual or close friendships • dating • leisure activities • degree of freedom from parental authority and intrusion
School (where applicable)	• time in school • changes of school • attendance record • work record • behaviour in relation to staff and peers • bullying
Problems and coping strategies	• current problem behaviours, eg delinquency • anxieties, eg school, running away, physical, sexual or emotional abuse • alcohol or drug abuse

General health	• previous significant medical history
	• present health status
	• psychiatric status including specifically:
	  – variation in sleep patterns
	  – appetite
	  – mood
	• health contacts, eg GP, clinic or hospital appointments
	• current treatments

Family structure and relationships	• marital status of parents • composition of family • rating of relationships within the family • emotional climate in the home • expressed emotions (EE) • frequency and pattern of arguments • past or present abuse

Family circumstances	<ul><li>level of income</li><li>housing</li><li>environmental problems</li><li>family pathology, eg crime, mental illness</li><li>family history of suicide</li><li>physical or mental disability</li><li>contacts with social agencies</li></ul>
Other higher risk items	<ul><li>others not present or nearby at the time</li><li>intervention unlikely</li><li>precautions taken against discovery</li><li>suicide note</li><li>problems for longer than a month</li><li>episode planned for more than three hours</li><li>feeling hopeless about the future</li><li>feeling sad most of the time prior to the act of DSH</li><li>contributing social or family adversity</li><li>use of alcohol or drugs</li></ul>

(Chapter 11, paragraph 11.20)

CHECK-LIST 8

Questions Relating to
Suicide Risk in Adolescents

A.	**Does this patient have the potential for self-harm?**	Here the question has to do with whether the patient presents with one or more risk factors in his or her history or current life experience. For example, is there a family history of suicide, or has the patient been exposed to the suicidal behaviour of a peer?
B.	**Might this person possibly harm himself or herself?**	The possibility of suicide increases substantially where there is evidence that death or suicide is on the individual's mind. Additional factors here are cognitive rigidity, and evidence of social isolation or alienation.
C.	**If self-harm is possible, what is the probability of such behaviour, and what are the circumstances, the degree of lethality and imminence involved?**	Whether suicidal intent will be acted upon depends on a number of situational factors, including conditions of threat or stress, the availability or accessibility of method, and often a particular trigger or event which has a high level of personal meaning for the individual.
D.	**Are there continuing provocative factors?**	The individual's living circumstances need to be considered, in particular whether there are any deficits in care and supervision.

(Chapter 11, paragraph 11.27)

CHECK-LIST 9

The Green Card
(used following DSH)

Instructions on how to use this card

This card explains how to get immediate help from the hospital if, in the future, you feel despairing, unable to cope or have thoughts of harming yourself.

At any time of the day or night, a doctor in psychiatry is available to speak to you on the phone, or see you in person at the hospital.

The doctor will discuss your problem with you and tell you how he or she can help. If you would like a break from home to help put your problem in perspective, the doctor will arrange for you to stay on one of our wards overnight.

Important

You must contact the doctor on duty **instead** of harming yourself if he or she is to help you.

If you have **already** harmed yourself (eg by an overdose), the doctor will have to refer you straight to the Casualty Department. This is because you may have put your physical health at risk.

Keep this card on you, eg in your wallet or handbag. If you do lose it, you can get a replacement from your GP.

If you need help, either -

1. **Telephone** the number on the front of this card and ask for extension XXX (this will put you through to a unit at the Hospital).
2. Ask to speak to the **nurse in charge**.
3. Say that you have a **green card** and would like to speak to the **doctor on duty**. (You need not give your name if you don't want to).
4. The nurse will take your number and ask the doctor to phone you back as soon as possible.

or:

1. **Go in person** to the **Accident and Emergency Department** of the Hospital.
2. Show the last page of this card to the **receptionist** and say that you would like to see the **doctor on duty**.
3. The receptionist will show you where you can wait, and will call the doctor for you.

(Chapter 14, paragraph 14.9)

CHECK-LIST 10

Advantages and Limitations
of Community Care

Advantages

- With support from the therapist, the patient can use and improve coping skills to deal with relevant stressors in a normal environment (as opposed to escaping from stressors which may occur as a result of hospitalisation).
- The patient may prefer it: he or she may suffer less stigmatisation and less reduction in self-esteem – both of which can be problems arising from hospitalisation.
- The patient does not lose contact with his or her family, usual carers and normal environment.
- The patient retains his or her usual life-style, autonomy and responsibilities.
- The therapist generally has easier access to relevant family dynamics and other contributing stressors which can then be addressed more directly.

Limitations

- It is more difficult to ensure safety in terms of close supportive care and safe environment.
- It is more difficult to ensure treatment compliance.
- It is more difficult to monitor physical and medical condition.
- It is more difficult to provide sanctuary from stressors (eg, may be exposed to intolerable family tension, social isolation or hostility).
- Family or carers may be placed under undue strain/burden of care or may be perceived to be so by the patient.

(Chapter 7, paragraph 7.9)

CHECK-LIST 11

Factors Favouring Community Management of People at Risk of Suicide

Patient Variables

- Suicidal intent judged to be at a manageable level.

- Good rapport with patient established.

- Patient able to agree a treatment contract or give a commitment not to harm self.

- Good social supports available (especially if a 24-hour presence can be provided).

- No history of impulsive behaviour.

- Alcohol or drug intake, if relevant, under adequate control.

- No serious suicide attempts in the recent past.

- Compliant with management plan.

- Stressors in home setting at a manageable level.

- No physical complications.

- Patient's preference is to be treated at home rather than in hospital.

- Patient has skills in independent living and adequate housing and financial resources.

Therapist/Professional Variables

- Adequate psychiatric training.

- Confident in dealing with psychological problems.

- Sufficient time to allow regular and flexible contacts.

- Back-up team available to provide support when key therapist not available.

- Appropriate prescription of medication (eg amount of drug prescribed and how frequently).

(Chapter 7, paragraph 7.10)

CHECK-LIST 12

Points Which Suggest Caution in Adopting a Community-Based Approach

- Patient not known previously.

- Lack of corroborative information (eg from relative or friend or other hospitals).

- Limited documentation (eg self-referral, no GP letter).

- Previous history of significant suicide risk.

- High risk clinical syndrome (depression, alcohol or substance abuse, psychotic illness, impulsive personality disorder).

- Recent episode of serious DSH, especially if of life endangering severity and planned.

- Continuing suicidal ideas, especially if the patient cannot give reassurance about safety.

- Impulsive behaviour.

- Recent alcohol or other substance abuse.

- Fluctuation in degree of distress, to such an extent that it is difficult to predict risk at all times.

- Insight and judgement impaired by psychotic ideation (eg depression, morbid self-blame and hopelessness in depression).

- Close empathic relationship not established (eg first interview, paranoid ideas and suspiciousness).

- Denial of suicidal ideas in spite of recent serious episode of DSH (the patient may not reveal true intent).

- Alienation of patient from others because of difficult behaviour or recurrent relapse.

- Difficulty in accepting or utilising available forms of help.

- Morbid ideas which refer to others, eg relatives included in depressive ideas of futility and hopelessness.

- Adverse and unresolved socio-demographic factors, particularly awaited events such as a court appearance.

(Chapter 7, paragraph 7.13)

CHECK-LIST 13

Management of People at Risk of Suicide in the Community

The therapist should:

1. Set frequency of visits.

2. Explain what will happen.

3. Address obstacles, eg work, transport, anxiety about attending.

4. Decide who will see the patient and introduce them appropriately.

5. Make it clear how the patient can contact other agencies when the surgery or mental health centre is closed and discuss this in detail, giving telephone numbers.

6. Plan activity up to next appointment.

7. Consider the appropriateness of a problem-solving approach.

8. Aim at establishing a supportive relationship at first interview.

9. Emphasise openness, acceptance, commitment and detailed identification of patient's difficulties and fears.

10. Emphasise the concept of an alliance with the patient, which aims to ward off and effectively deal with feelings of despair.

11. Include family and friends in the management plan, giving them time to talk about their fears and concerns, if necessary with a different therapist.

12. Identify specific strategies for dealing with the urge to commit suicide, eg talking to someone.

13. Examine current use of alcohol and non-prescribed drugs.

14. Make a list of reasons for living, constructed at times when the patient is feeling better.

15. Project forward towards the most difficult times likely to occur, identify them and think through ways of dealing with them.

16. Think about how to cope with unexpected difficulties.

17. Observe the principles of establishing a contract with commitment on both sides.

(Chapter 7, paragraph 7.15)

CHECK-LIST 14

Problems Encountered in the Management of
Patients at Risk of Suicide in Hospital

- Failure to gain admission.

- Danger times:

  a. Soon after admission (particular care should be exercised when there has been impulsive, agitated behaviour).
  b. Between staff shifts.
  c. Patient leave.
  d. Bank holidays, staff leave, or other time of disrupted routine.
  e. Discharge: may be premature.
  f. Follow-up period.

- Physical hazards in hospital environment.

- Adverse response to medication.

- Poor communication between staff.

- Lack of clear code of practice in the care of suicidal people.

- Failure to involve key others in treatment process.

- Poor technique in assessing and monitoring risk.

- Misleading clinical improvement.

- Terminal progressive alienation of patient.

(Chapter 8, paragraph 8.42)

CHECK-LIST 15

Core Knowledge and Skills
Relevant to the Training of Professionals who Work with
People at Risk of Suicide

- Basic knowledge of psychiatric conditions, particularly the many presentations of depressive illness and more minor conditions.

- Models of suicidal behaviour, antecedents, process and prognosis.

- Monitoring and assessment, with particular reference to severity and risk.

- Methodologies for responding to an emergency.

- The professional and personal resources needed in managing crises.

- Therapeutic interventions including brief, focused work, and the indications for longer-term involvement.

- Multidisciplinary working, managing conflict in attitudes, opinions and beliefs.

- The role of voluntary agencies in monitoring and support.

(Chapter 16, paragraph 16.9)

CHECK-LIST 16

Key elements underpinning good commissioning

- Strategy

- Effectiveness through contracting

- Developing the knowledge base

- Responsiveness to the population

- Partnerships with providers

- Healthy alliances

- Organisational fitness, ie improving the skills and attitudes of managers

(Chapter 18, paragraph 18.1)

CHECK-LIST 17

Strategic Measures Which Purchasers Might Take

Measures to improve quality and efficiency of Services

- Establish multidisciplinary audit meetings on suicide and DSH.

- Establish or contribute to local prison suicide prevention groups.

- Ensuring through contracts, new, or improved, observation policies on key wards.

- Establish a district or locality-based suicide prevention group.

- Ensure that all providers with whom they contract are implementing the care programme approach and supervision registers.

Measures to promote prevention and early intervention services

- Commission a specialist aftercare service for people who deliberately harm themselves.

- Encourage providers to prioritise training for all staff dealing with people who deliberately harm themselves or are at high risk of suicide.

- Produce specialist information and support to vulnerable occupational groups, such as farmers.

- Ensure that arrangements exist for the prompt and sensitive assessment of adolescents who deliberately harm themselves.

- Establish a database for data collection on vulnerable groups of people.

(Chapter 18, paragraph 18.2)

CHECK-LIST 18

Knowledge Base for Commissioners

- Resource allocation.

- Quality management and resources.

- Appropriate outcome measures.

- Evaluating different approaches to contracting.

- Population-based health assessment.

- Methodology for priority setting.

- Cost-effectiveness of services.

- Cost-effectiveness of interventions.

(Chapter 18, paragraph 18.11)

CHECK-LIST 19

Key Elements for Mental Health Services Contracts

- Full implementation of the care programme approach as well as monitoring and reporting arrangements.

- The maintenance and development of a mental health information system, including supervision registers.

- Staff adequately trained in the care programme approach and in risk assessment and management.

- Suitable arrangements for the management and clinical supervision of staff in community mental health teams.

- Audit of suicides.

- Agreed procedures in the event of a homicide or assault by a patient subject to the care programme approach.

- An agreed statement or protocol describing how suicidal adolescents will receive inpatient care.

(Chapter 18, paragraph 18.4)

CHECK-LIST 20

The Basic Principles for Successful Inter-agency Working

- an understanding that collaboration is a means to an end, namely improved quality and outcome for service users.

- shared values and principles between organisations (or an understanding and recognition of where these differ to enable negotiation).

- structural mechanisms that are set within a context of informal networking and relationships.

- a planning process that reflects the priorities of the senior levels of management and couples them to the working experience of staff at the grassroots of the organisations.

- an agreed language that allows honest discussion of different positions rather than tokenistic acceptance of superficial ideology.

- clear specification of the task and the timescale within which it will be achieved.

- appropriate and committed representation that is empowered to take decisions or reflect the decision making process of the organisation.

- access, if possible, to a joint or jointly committed budget.

(Chapter 18, paragraph 18.17)

CHECK-LIST 21

Issues to be Considered in Evaluating the Quality of Services for Persons at Risk of Suicide

Is the philosophy of care appropriate and understood by all concerned?	The aims of the service should be understood by all working in it. Positive attitudes to suicide prevention should be encouraged and negative attitudes addressed. The role of relatives and key others in both assessment and management should be recognised, and at the same time, the rights and autonomy of the individual acknowledged.
Is there a balanced range of interventions available?	These should include psychological, social, and physical treatments, in community and hospital settings.
Do staff possess the necessary skills and is there provision for updating these skills as appropriate?	Skilled interview techniques are vital. The procedures for well-defined supportive observation should be thoroughly understood, as should the effect of drugs both in terms of side-effects which may affect the patient's mood, and toxicity in overdose. Regular training in basic resuscitation should be available and there should be provision for on-going training and education for all staff.
Are staffing levels adequate?	There should be sufficient trained staff available at all times, including weekends, holidays and times of staff changeover. More specialist help should be available as required, especially to those staff working in the community.
Does the service make itself available to those who need its help?	A good service acts in alliance with other agencies, such as social services departments, the Prison Service and voluntary bodies such as the Samaritans, and will have good working relations with them, offering advice and support. It will reach out to those at greater risk.
Are there clear operational guidelines for community-based care?	Guidelines should be readily available in each unit and fully understood by all persons involved in patient care. These should include a clear indication of the degree of severity of risk beyond which this type of treatment is neither practicable not appropriate.

Can those working in the community commit the necessary time to the task?	This is vital to good community based services. Where sufficient time cannot be committed, other approaches should be considered. The time commitment should be covered in operational guidelines on community-based care.
In the hospital setting, are sufficient beds available to allow for the admission of all those who require inpatient care?	The phenomenon of misleading improvement, and the consequent risk of premature discharge should be recognised.
Is there adequate provision for appropriate treatment of people who deliberately harm themselves?	There should be provision for urgent specialist assessment of DSH cases in Accident and Emergency Departments and arrangements for admission to the appropriate inpatient facilities where necessary. If admission to a medical ward is necessary, there should be locally-agreed procedures for obtaining a full psychiatric assessment and medical staff should know how to obtain psychiatric advice.
Is the inpatient ward milieu appropriate for the care of suicidal people?	It is important that the ward should be seen by patients as a non-threatening environment which is free as far as possible from disturbance. There should be facilities for intensive, supportive observation, when necessary.
Does the service offer support to relatives and key others, especially to those suffering bereavement after the suicide of someone close to them?	Suicide brings a trail of emotional devastation to others and a good service will recognise and cater for their needs as well as those of the individual at risk.
Are there appropriate facilities for adolescents and other distinctive vulnerable groups?	The distinctive needs of adolescents should be addressed (see Chapter 11 and also Check-List 22 p126) The needs of vulnerable groups should be reflected in the pattern of services available.

Are there good lines of communication between all elements of the service?	All relevant information should be obtained and documented so that no important factor is missed. Proper documentation ensures that those in contact with an individual at risk have all the information necessary to make decisions. Information should flow between all levels of service and between all agencies involved.

(Chapter 15, paragraph 15.13)

CHECK-LIST 22

Issues to be Considered in Evaluating the
Quality of Services for Adolescents

Is there provision for the full assessment and treatment of a young person who exhibits one of the risk factors for suicide?	This should include provision for those with depressive disorders, those who misuse alcohol or drugs and for those with severe anti-social behaviour. In particular, it is important to identify whether there are professionals who are able to identify depression in young people and treat it vigorously.
Are there local health promotion policies which address the needs of adolescents?	These should include policies targeted at especially vulnerable groups, such as homeless young people and those in the care of the local authority.
Is there provision for the full assessment of a young person following an act of DSH?	It is important to ensure that there is provision for younger adolescents to be admitted overnight to medical wards for observation and interview even when they do not obviously need physical resuscitation. There should be local guidelines that ensure that this happens.
Can the assessment of young people who have been admitted be undertaken in adequate privacy?	This is important if the full background is to be established.
Are there professionals available who have the appropriate training in the assessment of suicide risk and personal safety in adolescents?	Professionals should have the ability to identify psychiatric disorder which requires treatment and should be well informed as to local resources in both the statutory and voluntary sectors. They should be aware of which services and agencies are likely to be most acceptable to this age group.
Do local prescribing policies allow local psychiatrists to prescribe anti-depressants which are minimally toxic in overdose?	It is important to prevent hoarding as far as possible.

Are there local guidelines for the management of young people who harm themselves and are these subject to clinical audit?	Clinical audit protocols and programmes should recognise the specific characteristics of this age group.
Are there sufficient treatment resources for psychiatric disorders and family disturbances which may have been revealed by assessment?	These should include both specialised mental health resources and less intensive but accessible community primary care and counselling services. It is important that these primary care and counselling services are appropriate for young people.
Are there arrangements for suicidal adolescents to be admitted promptly to an appropriate adolescent psychiatric ward or unit?	The unit needs to be sufficiently local to enable other family members to participate in treatment. Each health authority should have a contract with such a specialist unit.
Is there clear evidence of good communication between emergency services (Accident and Emergency or Casualty Departments), adolescent mental health services, general practitioners and, where appropriate, community paediatricians, school doctors, and social services?	There should be adequate liaison between all these groups, which is supported by appropriately flexible relationships based on mutual understanding of the needs of adolescents and young people.

(Chapter 11, paragraph 11.39)

PART F

BIBLIOGRAPHY

Bibliography

The bibliography contains the full references to all documents cited in the text. Additional documents and papers, which are not specifically referred to in the text, are also contained. The intention is to provide sources of further information for interested readers.

American Psychiatric Association (1987). Diagnostic and Statistical Manual of Mental Disorders, Third Edition, Revised. Washington, DC: American Psychiatric Association.

Anderson, L., (1981). Notes on the linkage between the sexually abused child and the suicidal adolescent. Journal of Adolescence, **4**, 15-16.

Backett, S., (1988). Suicide and prevention: stress in prison. In Imprisonment Today: current issues in the Prison Debate. Backett, S., McNeil, J. and Yellowlees, A. (eds). London: MacMillan.

Barraclough, B.M., Bunch, J., Nelson, B. and Sainsbury, P., (1974). A hundred cases of suicide: clinical aspects. British Journal of Psychiatry, **125**, 355-373.

Barraclough, B.M., Shepperd, D.M., Jennings, C., (1977). Do newspaper reports of Coroners' inquests incite people to commit suicide? British Journal of Psychiatry, **150**, 528-532.

Barraclough, B.M., (1980). Suicide and epilepsy. In Symposium on Psychiatric Aspects of Epilepsy. Reynolds, E. A. and Trimble, M. (eds). London: Churchill Livingstone.

Beck, A.T., Steer, R.A., Kovacs, M. and Garrison, B., (1985). Hopelessness and eventual suicide. A ten year prospective study of patients hospitalised with suicidal ideation. American Journal of Psychiatry, **145**, 559-563.

Beck, A.T., Schuyler, D. and Herman, J., (1974). Development of suicidal intent scales. In The Prediction of Suicide. Beck, A.T., Resnick, H.L.P. and Lettieri, D.J. (eds). Bowie, (Maryland): Charles Press Publishers.

Beck, A.T., Rush, A. J., Shaw, B. and Emery, G., (1979). Cognitive theory of depression. New York: Guildford Press.

Berman, A.L. and Jobes, D.A., (1991). Adolescent Suicide: Assessment and Interventions. Washington DC: American Psychological Association.

Bingham, C.R., Bennion, L., Openshaw, D. and Adams, G.R., (1994). An analysis of age, gender, and racial differences in recent national trends of youth suicide. Journal of Adolescence, **17**, 53-72.

Birleson, P., (1980). Teenage suicide. Journal of Maternal and Child Health, **5, 6,** 238-245.

Black, M., Erulkar, J., Kerfoot, M., Meadow, R. and Baderman, H., (1992). The management of parasuicide in young people under 16. Bulletin of the Royal College of Psychiatrists, **6,** 182-185.

Brent, D., (1987). Correlates of medical lethality of suicide attempts in children and adolescents. Journal of the American Academy of Child and Adolescent Psychiatry, **26,** 87-91.

Bibliography

Brent, D., Perper, J., Goldstein, C.E., Kolko, D., Allan, M.S., Allman, C. and Zelenak, J., (1986). Risk factors for adolescent suicide. A comparison of adolescent suicide victims with suicidal inpatients. Archives of General Psychiatry, **45,** 581-588.

Buckstein, O. G., Brent, D. A., Perper, G. A., Moritz, G., Baugher, M., Shweers, J., Roth, C., Balach, L. (1993). Risk factors for completed suicide among adolescents with a lifetime history of substance abuse: a case-control study. Acta Psychiatrica Scandinavica.

Buglass, D. and Horton, J., (1974). The repetition of parasuicide: a comparison of three cohorts. British Journal of Psychiatry, **125,** 168-174.

Bulletin of the Royal College of Psychiatrists (1982). The management of parasuicide in young people under 16, **6,** 182-185.

Charlton, J., Kelly, S., Dunnell, K., Evans, B., Jenkins, R. and Wallis, R., (1992). Trends in suicide deaths in England and Wales. Populaton Trends, No.69 (Autumn), 10-16. London: OPCS, HMSO.

Charlton, J., Kelly, S., Dunnell, K., Evans, B. and Jenkins, R., (1993). Suicide deaths in England and Wales: Trends in factors associated with suicide deaths. Population Trends, No.71, 34-42. London: OPCS, HMSO.

Center For Disease Control, (1986). Youth suicide in the US, 1970-1980. Department of Health and Human Services.

Coney, S., (1993). New Zealand: youth suicide. The Lancet, **341,** 683.

Crossman, R., (1977). The Diaries of a Cabinet Minister. Vol.III. London: Hamish Hamilton.

Deakin, E.Y., (1986). Adolescent suicidal and self-destructive behaviour: an intervention study. In Suicide and Depression among Adolescents and Young Adults. Klerman, G. (ed). Washington DC: American Psychiatric Press Inc.

Delamothe, T., (1993). Wanted: guidelines that doctors will follow. British Medical Journal, **307,** 218.

Department of Health, (1990). The care programme approach for people with a mental illness referred to the special psychiatric services. (HC(90)23, LASSL(90)11).

Department of Health, (1992). The Health of the Nation: A Strategy for Health in England. London: HMSO.

Department of Health, (1993). The Health of the Nation: Key Area Handbook Mental Illness. London: HMSO.

Department of Health, (1993). Working Together for Better Health. London: HMSO.

Department of Health, (1993). Research for Health. London: HMSO.

Department of Health and NHS Management Executive (1994). Introduction of supervision registers for mentally ill people from 1 April 1994. Health Service guidelines, HSG(94)5.

DHSS, Health Services Management. The management of deliberate self-harm.

Diekstra, R.F., (1989). Suicidal behaviour in adolescents and young adults: the international picture. Crisis, **10,** 16-35.

Dooley, E., (1990). Prison suicides in England and Wales 1972-1987. British Journal of Psychiatry, **156,** 40-45.

Eisenberg, L. Public policy: risk factor or remedy? In Risk Factors and the Prevention of Child Psychiatric Disorders. Shaffer, D., Phillips, I., Enzer, N. (eds). Washington DC: ADAMHA.

Farberow, N.L. and MacKinnon, D., (1974). A suicide prevention schedule for neuropsychiatric hospital patients. Journal of Nervous and Mental Diseases, **158,** 408-419.

Fawcett, J., Scheftner, W.A., Fogg, L., Clark, D.C., Young, M.A., Hedeker, D. and Gibbons, R., (1990). Time-related predictors of suicide in major affective disorders. American Journal of Psychiatry, **147,** 1189-1194.

Fishbein, M. and Ajzeu, I., (1975). Belief, attitude, intention and behaviour: an introduction to theory and research. (Reading Mass) Addison-Wesley.

Fraser, S.G., (1986). Interpersonal problem-solving training and suicidal behaviour. British Journal of Cognitive Psychotherapy, **4,** 39-47.

Gallagher, A. and Sheehy, N. Suicide in rural communities. Journal of Community and Applied Social Psychology (in press).

Gardner, R., (1991). Guidelines on the clinical management of suicidal patients in hospital. Cambridge Mental Health Services. Addenbrooks Hospital, Cambridge.

Garland, A., Shaffer, D. and Whittle, B., (1989). A survey of youth suicide prevention programmes. Journal of the American Academy of Child and Adolescent Psychiatry, **28,** 931-934.

Garland, A. and Zigler, E., (1993). Adolescent suicide prevention: current research and social policy implications. American Psychologist, **48,** 169-182.

Garrison, C.Z., McKeown, R.E., Valois, R.F. and Vincent M.L., (1993). Aggression, substance use, and suicidal behaviours in high school students. American Journal of Public Health, **83,** 179-184.

Gasquet, I. and Choquet, M., (1993). Gender role in adolescent suicidal behaviour: observations and therapeutic implications. Acta Psychiatrica Scandinavia, **87, i,** 59-65.

Goh, S.E., Salmons, P.H. and Whittington, R.M., (1989). Suicide in psychiatric hospitals. British Journal of Psychiatry, **154,** 247-250.

Goldacre, M., Seagrott, V. and Hawton, K., (1993). Suicide after discharge from psychiatric care. The Lancet, **342,** 283-286.

Gould, M.S. and Shaffer, D., (1986). The impact of suicide in television movies: evidence of imitation. New England Journal of Medicine, **315,** 690-694.

Gould, M.S., Shaffer, D. and Davies, M., (1990). Truncated pathways from childhood: attrition in follow-up studies due to death. In Straight and Devious Pathways from Childhood to Adulthood. Robins, L. and Rutter, M., (eds). Cambridge: Cambridge University Press.

Greenblatt, M. and Robertson, M.J., (1993). Lifestyles, adaptive strategies, and sexual behaviours of homeless adolescents. Hospital and Community Psychiatry, **44,** 12, 1177-1180.

Greening, L. and Dollinger, F., (1993). Rural adolescents: perceived personal risks of suicide. Journal of Youth and Adolescence, **22.**

Handy, S., Chithiramohan, R., Ballard, C. and Silveira, W., (1991). Ethnic differences in adolescent self-poisoning: a comparison of Asian and Caucasian groups. Journal of Adolescence, **14,** 157-162.

Harrington, R.C. and Dyer, E., (1993). Suicide and attempted suicide in adolescents. Current Opinion in Psychiatry, **6,** 467-469.

Hart, W.A., (1993). Deliberate self-harm is under-reported. British Medical Journal, **307,** 805.

Hawley, C.J., James, D.V., Birkett, P.L., Baldwin, D.G., deRuiter, M.J. and Priest R.G., (1991). Suicidal ideation as a presenting complaint: associated diagnoses and characteristics in a casualty population. British Journal of Psychiatry, **159,** 232-238.

Hawton, K., Osborne, M., O'Grady J. and Cole, D., (1982). Classification of adolescents who take overdoses. British Journal of Psychiatry, **140,** 124-131.

Hawton, K. and Catalan, J., (1987). Attempted Suicide: A Practical Guide to its Nature and Management. Oxford: Oxford University Press.

Hawton, K., Fagg, J., McKeown, S.P., (1989). Alcoholism, alcohol, and attempted suicide. Alcohol, **24,** 3-9.

Hawton, K. and Fagg, J., (1992). Deliberate self-poisoning and self-injury in adolescents: a study of characteristics and trends in Oxford, 1976-1989. British Journal of Psychiatry, **161,** 816-823.

Hawton, K., (1992). By their own young hand. British Medical Journal, **304,** 1000.

Hazell, P., (1991). Postvention after teenage suicide: an Australian experience. Journal of Adolescence, **14,** 335-342.

Hill, J.P. and Lynch, M.E., (1983). The intensification of gender-related role expectations during early adolescence. In Girls At Puberty. Brooks-Gunn, J. and Peterson, A. (eds). New York: Plenum Press.

Hill, P., (1989). Adolescent Psychiatry. Edinburgh: Churchill Livingstone.

Hoberman, H.M. and Garfinkel, B.D., (1988). Completed suicide in youth. Canadian Journal of Psychiatry, **33,** 494-504.

Kalafet, J. and Elias, M., (1992). Adolescents' experience with and response to suicidal peers. Suicidal life threat. Behaviour, **22,** 3, 315-321.

Kerfoot, M., (1987). Family therapy and psychotherapy following suicidal behaviour by young adolescents. In Suicide in Adolescence. Diekstra, R. and Hawton, K. (eds). Dordrecht: Martinus Nijhoff.

Kerfoot, M., (1988). Deliberate self-poisoning in childhood and early adolescence. Journal of Child Psychology and Psychiatry, **29,** 335-334.

Kerfoot, M. and McHugh, B., (1992). The outcome of childhood suicidal behaviour. Acta Paedopsychiatrica, **55,** 3, 141-145.

Kerfoot, M., Harrington, R., Dyer, E., (1995). Brief home-based intervention with young suicide attempters and their families. Journal of Adolescence, **18,** 557-568.

King, C.A., Hill, E.M., Naylor, M. et al, (1993). Alcohol consumption in relation to other predictors of suicidality among adolescent inpatient girls. Journal of the American Academy of Child and Adolescent Psychiatry, **32,** 82-88.

Kingsbury, S., (1993). Parasuicide in adolescence: a message in a bottle. Association for Child Psychology and Psychiatry Review and Newsletter, **15,** 253-259.

Kingsbury, S., (1994). The psychological and social characteristics of Asian adolescent overdose. Journal of Adolescence, **17,** 131-136.

Klingman, A. and Hochdorf, Z., (1993). Coping with distress and self-harm: the impact of a primary prevention programme among adolescents. Journal of Adolescence, **16,** 121-140.

Kotila, L. and Lonngvist, J., (1989). Suicide and violent death among suicide attempters. Acta Psychiatrica Scandinavia, **79,** 453-459.

Kovacs, M., Goldston, D. and Gatsonis, C., (1993). Suicidal behaviours and childhood - onset depressive disorders: a longitudinal investigation. Journal of the American Academy of Child and Adolescent Psychiatry, **32,** 8-20.

Lerner, M. and Clum, G., (1990). Treatment of suicide ideators: a problem-solving approach. Behaviour Therapy, **21,** 403-311.

Liebling, A., (1992). Suicide in Prison. London: Routledge.

Liebling, A., (1993). Suicides in young prisoners: a summary. Death Studies, **17, 5,** 381-409.

Marttunen, M.J., Aro, H.M., Lonngvist, J.K., (1992). Adolescent suicide: end-point of long-term difficulties. Journal of the American Academy of Child and Adolescent Psychiatry, **31,** 649-654.

Marttunen, M.J., Aro, H.M., Lonngvist, J.K., (1993). Adolescents and suicide: a review of psychological autopsy studies. European Child and Adolescent Psychiatry, **2,** 10-18.

McClure, G.M., (1986). Recent changes in suicide among adolescents in England and Wales. Journal of Adolescence, **9,** 135-144.

McClure, G.M., (1988). Suicide in children in England And Wales. Journal of Child Psychology and Psychiatry, **29, 3,** 345-349.

Merrill, J. and Owens, J., (1986). Ethnic differences in self-poisoning: a comparison of Asian and Caucasian groups. British Journal of Psychiatry, **148,** 708-712.

Metha, A., (1988). The relationship between adolescent fatal suicide and adolescent attempted suicide: A problem of prediction.

Miles, C.P., (1977). Conditions predisposing to suicide: a review. Journal of Nervous and Mental Disease, **164,** 231-246.

Morgan, H.G., (1979). Death wishes? The Understanding and Management of Deliberate Self-Harm. Chichester. John Wiley.

Morgan, H.G. and Priest, P., (1991). Suicide and other unexpected deaths among psychiatric patients. British Journal of Psychiatry, **158,** 368-374.

Morgan, H.G., Jones, E.M. and Owen, J.H., (1993). Secondary prevention of non-fatal deliberate self-harm. The Green Card study. British Journal of Psychiatry, **163,** 111-113.

Morgan, H.G., (1994). Clinical audit of suicide and other unexpected deaths. NHS Management Executive.

Morgan, H.G., Evans, M., (1994). How negative are we to the idea of suicide prevention? Journal of the Royal Society of Medicine. **87,** 622-625.

Morgan, H.G., Evans, M., Johnson, C. and Stanton, R. (1996). Can a lecture influence attitudes to suicide prevention? Journal of the Royal Society of Medicine, **89,** 87-90.

Motto, J.A., (1967). Suicide and suggestibility – the role of the press. American Journal of Psychiatry, **124,** 2, 252-256.

Motto, J.A. and Heilbron, D.C., (1976). Development and validation of scales for estimation of suicidal risk. In Suicidology, Contemporary Developments. Shneidman, E.S. (ed). New York: Grune and Stratton.

Murphy, G.E. and Wetzel, R.D., (1990). The lifetime risk of suicide in alcoholism. Archives of General Psychiatry, **47,** 383-392.

National Mental Health Association, (1986). Commission on the prevention of Mental-Emotional Disabilities. Alexandria, VA: National Mental Health Association.

News, Suicide. British Medical Journal, 1994, **308,** 7-11.

NHS Health Advisory Service, (1993). A Unique Window on Change. The Annual Report of the Director for 1992-93. London: HMSO.

NHSME, (1993). Purchasing for Health – a framework for action. London: HMSO.

Nordentoft, M., Breun, L., Munck, L.K., Nordestgaard, A.J., Hunding, A. and Bjaeldager, P.A.L., (1993). High mortality by natural and unnatural causes: a ten year follow up study of patients admitted to a poisoning treatment centre after suicide attempts. British Medical Journal, **306,** 1637-1641.

Office of Population Census and Surveys, (1990). Mortality Statistics. Cause: England and Wales. London: HMSO.

Ollendick, T.H., Mattis, S.G., and King, N.J., (1994). Panic in children and adolescents: a review. Journal of Child Psychology and Psychiatry, **35, 1**, 113-134.

Pallis, D.J., Barraclough, B.M., Levey, A.B., Jenkins, J.S. and Sainsbury, P., (1982). Estimating suicide risk among attempted suicides – the development of new clinical scales. British Journal of Psychiatry, **141,** 37-44.

Paykel, E.G. and Priest, R.G., (1992). Recognition and management of depression in general practice; Consensus Statement. British Medical Journal, **305,** 1198-1202.

Pfeffer, C.R., Klerman, G.L., Hurt, S.W., Kakuma, T., Peskin, J.R. and Siefker, C.A., (1993). Suicidal children grown up: rates and psychosocial risk factors for suicide attempts during follow-up. Journal of the American Academy of Adolescent Psychiatry, **32, 1,** 106-113.

Phillips, D.P., (1974). The influence of suggestion on suicide: substantive and theoretical implications of the Werther effect. American Sociology Review, **39,** 340-354.

Pritchard, C., (1992). Is there a link between suicide in young men and unemployment: a comparison of the UK with other European Community countries. British Journal of Psychiatry, **160,** 750-756.

Rao, U., Weissman, M.M., Martin, J.A. and Hammond, R.W., (1993). Childhood depression and risk of suicide: preliminary report of a longitudinal study. Journal of the American Academy of Child and Adolescent Psychiatry, **32,** 21-27.

Reder, P., Lucey, C. and Fredman, J., (1991). The challenge of deliberate self-harm by young adolescents. Journal of Adolescence, **14,** 135-148.

Rich, C.L., Young, D. and Fowler, R.C., (1986). San Diego suicide study I: young vs old subjects. Archives of General Psychiatry, **43,** 577-582.

Richman, J., (1986). Family Therapy For Suicidal People. New York: Springer.

Rinsza, M.E., Berg, R.A. and Locke, C., (1988). Sexual abuse, somatic and emotional reactions. Child Abuse and Neglect, **12,** 201-208.

Rotheram-Borus, M. J., Piacentini, J., Miller, S., Graae, F., Castro-Blanco, D., (1994). Brief cognitive-behavioural treatment for adolescent suicide attempters and their families. Journal of the American Academy of Child and Adolescent Psychiatry, **33,** 508-517.

Royal College of Psychiatrists, (1993). Prevention In Psychiatry. Council Report CR 21.

Royal College of Psychiatrists, Royal College of General Practitioners and Wendy Lloyd Audio Productions Ltd., (1994). Coping with Depression.

Seager, C.P. and Flood, R.A., (1965). Suicide in Bristol. British Journal of Psychiatry, **111,** 919-932.

Shaffer, D., (1974). Suicide in childhood and early adolescence. Journal of Child Psychology and Psychiatry, **15,** 275-291.

Shaffer, D. and Gould, M., (1987). A Study Of Completed and Attempted Suicide in Adolescents (Progress Report, Grant Number MH38198) Rockville, MD: National Institute of Mental Health.

Shaffer, D., Garland, A., Gould, M., Fisher, P. and Trautmann, P., (1988). Preventing teenage suicide: a critical review. Journal of the American Academy of Child and Adolescent Psychiatry, **27,** 675-687.

Shaffer, D., (1988). The epidemiology of teen suicide: an examination of risk factors. Journal of Clinical Psychiatry, **49,** 35-41.

Shaffer, D., Garland, A., Fisher, P., Bacon, K. and Vieland, V., (1990). Suicide crisis centres: a critical reappraisal with special reference to the prevention of youth suicide. In Preventing Mental Health Disturbances In Childhood, Goldston, S.E., Yager, J., Heinicke, C.N. and Pynoos, R.S. (eds). American Psychiatric Press Inc.

Shaffer, D., Garland, A., Vieland, V., Underwood, M. and Busner, C., (1991). The impact of curriculum-based suicide prevention programmes for teenagers. Journal of the American Academy of Child and Adolescent Psychiatry, **30,** 588-596.

Shaffer, D., (1993). Suicide and Suicide Prevention. Paper delivered to the Royal College of Psychiatrists Child and Adolescent Psychiatry Specialist Section Residential Meeting, University of Warwick.

Shafii, M., Steltz-Lenarsky, J., Derrick, A.M., Beckner, C. and Whittinghill, J.R., (1988). Comorbidity of mental disorders in the post-mortem diagnosis of completed suicide in children and adolescents. Journal of Affective Disorders, **15,** 227-233.

Shneidman, E.S., (1993). Suicide as Psychache: A Clinical Approach to Self-destructive Behaviour. Northvale, New Jersey: Jason Aaronson.

Spirito, A., Overholser, J. and Hart, K., (1989). Attempted suicide in adolescence: a review and critique of the literature. Clinical Psychology Review, **9,** 335-363.

Spivak, G. and Shure, M.B., (1974). Social Adjustment of Young Children. San Francisco, CA: Jossey-Bass.

Stone, N., (1993). Parental abuse as a precursor to childhood onset of depression and suicidality. Child Psychiatry and Human Development, **24/1,** 13-24.

Sudak, H.S., Ford, A., Rushforth, N. (eds) (1984). Suicide in the Young. Boston, Mass: John Wright.

Taylor, P.J., Burton, K., and Kolvin, I, (1992). Suicidal behaviour in children and adolescents. In: Recent Advances in Clinical Psychiatry. Granville Grossman K. (ed). Churchill Livingstone.

Tones, B.K. and Tilford (1994). Health Education Efficiency and Equity, Chapman Hall, London.

Trautmann, P. and Shaffer, D., (1984). Treatment of child and adolescent suicide attempters. In Suicide in the Young, Sudak, H.S., Ford, A.B., Rushforth, N.B. (eds). Boston: John Wright.

Trautmann, P.D., Stuart, N. and Morishima, N.A., (1993). Are adolescent suicide attempters non-compliant with out-patient care? Journal of the American Academy of Child and Adolescent Psychiatry, **32/1,** 89-94.

US Department of Health and Human Services, (1989). Report of the Secretary's Task Force on Youth Suicide. Washington DC: US Department of Health and Human Services.

Vassilas, C.A. and Morgan, H.G., (1993). General practitioners' contact with victims of suicide. British Medical Journal, **307,** 300-301.

Vieland, V., Whittle, B., Garland, A., Hicks, R. and Shaffer, D., (1991). The impact of curriculum-based suicide prevention programmes for teenagers: an 18-month follow-up. Journal of the American Academy of Child and Adolescent Psychiatry, **30,** 811-815.

Watts, D. and Morgan, H.G., (1994). Malignant alienation. British Journal of Psychiatry, **164,** 11-15.

Weiss, J.M.A., (1994). Suicide. In American Handbook of Psychiatry, 2nd Ed, II, 743-765.

Woolf, Lord Justice, (1991). Report Of An Enquiry Into The Prison Disturbances April 1990. Cmnd 1456. London: HMSO.

World Health Organisation, (1974). Suicide And Attempted Suicide. Public Health Papers No 58. Geneva: World Health Organisation.

Wright, A.F., (1993). Depression: Recognition and Management in General Practice. London: Royal College of General Practitioners.

Printed in the United Kingdom for HMSO
Dd 0302885   C25   7/96   210043   357611   29/35911